T0384067

Hospital Economics
A Primer on Resource Allocation to Improve Productivity & Sustainability

Hospital Economics
A Primer on Resource Allocation to Improve Productivity & Sustainability

A. Heri Iswanto

Routledge
Taylor & Francis Group

A PRODUCTIVITY PRESS BOOK

First published 2018
by Routledge
2 Park Square, Milton Park, Abingdon, Oxon OX14 4RN

and by Routledge
711 Third Avenue, New York, NY 10017

Routledge is an imprint of the Taylor & Francis Group, an informa business

British Library Cataloguing-in-Publication Data
A catalogue record for this book is available from the British Library

Library of Congress Cataloging-in-Publication Data
Names: Iswanto, A. Heri, 1977- author.
Title: Hospital economics : a primer on resource allocation to improve
productivity & sustainability / A. Heri Iswanto.
Description: Boca Raton : Taylor & Francis, 2018. | "A CRC title, part of the
Taylor & Francis imprint, a member of the Taylor & Francis Group, the
academic division of T&F Informa plc." | Includes bibliographical
references and index.
Identifiers: LCCN 2017051162| ISBN 9780815388777 (hardback : alk. paper) |
ISBN 9781351172523 (ebook)
Subjects: LCSH: Hospitals--Business management. | Hospitals--Administration.
Classification: LCC RA971.3 .I89 2018 | DDC 362.11068--dc23
LC record available at https://lccn.loc.gov/2017051162

ISBN: 978-0-815-38877-7 (hbk)
ISBN: 978-1-351-17252-3 (ebk)

Typeset in ITC Garamond Std Light
by Nova Techset Private Limited, Bengaluru & Chennai, India

To my loving wife, Shika,
and our children, Naya and Farrel

Contents

Acknowledgments

I want to praise the Almighty, Allah, SWT, for the mercy and blessings given so I could complete the book entitled *Hospital Economics*.

I extend special thanks to the colleagues who always give me motivation. My beloved wife, Shika Iswanto, who always supports me. My dears, Kannaya and Alfarrel, who have been waiting patiently and gave their time until the completion of this book.

I realize that this book is still far from being perfect. However, I have performed my best in presenting this book. Therefore, suggestions and criticism are always welcome for betterment. Finally, I hope that the book can be useful for hospital practitioners, academics in general, and especially those who want to conduct and perfect similar research.

Author

A. Heri Iswanto completed his Doctorate of Economic Science and Master and Bachelor in Hospital Management. As Deputy Dean of Academics in the Faculty of Health Science, University of Pembangunan National "Veteran" Jakarta, and as a lecturer at other universities in Jakarta, he has been the director at various hospitals including Prikasih, Lestari, and Kemang Medical Care. He has been a speaker at conferences and conducted training in the United States, Taiwan (ROC), IR Iran, Pakistan, Thailand, Malaysia, Singapore, Japan, China, the Philippines, and Vietnam.

Chapter 1

The Importance of Hospital Economics

Introduction

A health system in a country is a network that involves many
parties that are interconnected to one another. In a comprehensive public health network, at least 23 organizations, each of
which has contributed to the costs and benefits generated by
public health, are involved. The institutions involved in a universal health care system include, among others (CDC, 2013: 49):

1. *Schools.* Schools play a role in providing knowledge and
   training on health to the community to help people stay
   healthy and avoid diseases, such as by providing information on healthy lifestyles, especially to student groups in
   the community. Some schools specifically focus on education in the health field, such as nursing schools, medical
   schools, and so on.
2. *Mental health coaching institutions.* Institutions such as
   self-development centers, both religious and not, play a
   role in maintaining good mental health in the community.
   The majority of health problems can have their source in

mental problems (e.g., stress), and improvement in mental health quality can help reduce health problems.

3. *Governments.* Governments, both at the national and local levels, through the Ministry of Health and Health Service or nonministry institutions such as the National Agency of Drug and Food Control (BPOM), and even government agencies that are not directly related to health, have the role of regulation and supervision of aspects of public health related to the tasks and functions of each institution. For example, the Ministry of Housing has the role of ensuring houses occupied by people meet the standards of good health and do not cause disease for the residents. Overall, the role of the government is to build public health through health systems and partnerships with others in the health system through the principles of equality, solidarity, and justice-based human rights (WHO, 2006: 11).

4. *Emergency medical services.* These institutions include the Indonesian Red Cross (PMI) and various agencies of ambulance service providers that are able to respond quickly when people need emergency health care but are unable to reach the emergency room. These institutions provide first aid and emergency response in terms of housing, food, and health, including epidemic and mental health, for families and the whole community, in particular the vulnerable community, in order to return to normality after a crisis.

5. *Civilian groups.* Civilian groups are public institutions voluntarily established to provide health services in the community, as well as in the form of fundraising, such as cancer awareness groups, schizophrenia care groups, and so forth. The World Health Organization (WHO) registers at least 15 roles of civilian groups in the health sector, including service providers, who build a large public selection of health information, negotiate standards and public health approaches, promote pro-poor concerns

and social equity in resource allocation, and supervise the responsiveness and quality of health services (WHO, 2001: 6).

6. *Home care.* Home care includes various types of institutions specializing in the treatment of specific groups in the community. There are at least 15 types of institutions that exist in the community: child sanatorium (barriers to learning), day care (toddlers from 3 months to under 5 years), child care (fatherless/motherless children or orphans who are underprivileged and homeless), bina remaja (abandoned children dropping out of school), nursing homes for elders (old/seniors), bina daksa (physically disabled, other physical problems, and orthopedics), bina netra (vision impairment), bina rungu/wicara (speech defects/hearing impairment), bina grahita (mental impairment), bina laras (deviant behavior from the norm/ex-psychotic), bina pasca laras kronis (handicapped due to chronic diseases), marsudi putra/putri (brat), pamardi putra/i (former victims of drug abuse), karya wanita (prostitute), and bina karya (homeless or abandoned people) (Decree of Minister of Health No. 50/HUK/2004 on Social Institution Standardization and Social Institution Accreditation Guidelines). Part of the responsibility of a nursing home is to provide health care to the community members in their care.

7. *Association of physicians.* This group, particularly the Indonesian Doctors Association (IDI), is responsible for the health of the Indonesian nation.

8. *Law enforcement agencies.* Both military and police and other law enforcement agencies provide human security in various forms; one of them is health.

9. *Correctional facilities.* These institutions have expertise in teaching skills to people who break the law, including expertise in the field of health. In addition, the correctional facility has a role in the coaching of mental health in prison.

10. *Heads of state and local government* are responsible for providing shelter and managing various public areas, including the health sector.
11. *Emergency institutions* such as Search and Rescue (SAR), firefighters, the Indonesian National Board for Disaster Management, Badan Penanggulangan Bencana Daerah (BPBD) (Regional Disaster Management Agency), scouts, and so on, have proficiency in the health sector and are able to provide health assistance to the community.
12. *The Neighborhood Association (TNA) and Community Association (TCA)* as well as other organizations, coach the community in neighborhoods to be aware of various aspects of life, including health.
13. *Religious institutions* educate people to maintain health through the theories of the religion in which they believe.
14. *Integrated service posts* are at the center of basic health services for various strata of the community in the area.
15. *Community health centers* also become centers for primary health care for various strata of the community in the area.
16. *Employers/businesses,* both health and nonhealth businesses, are involved in community health. In the health sector, this includes pharmaceutical companies, drug stores, pharmacies, insurance companies, and clinics, while in the nonhealth sector, it includes almost all areas of business, which, of course, do not want the human resources they have to get sick.
17. *Youth and community organizations.* Most of these organizations have health care for their members, and there are some that focus on the public health.
18. *Nonprofit organizations* such as political parties, Badan Penyelenggara Jaminan Sosial (BPJS: Social Security Administering Body [SSAB]), and nongovernmental organizations (NGOs) have sections dedicated either entirely to health or as an effort to encourage support for them. Several political parties and NGOs have free ambulance services or even their own hospital.

19. *The household* is a leader in health care; that is, for the health of family members, at a minimum.
20. *Hospitals* provide a vital role in serving community members to achieve recovery.
21. *Treatment/rehabilitation centers* play a role in recovery from certain diseases or certain factors that cause disease, such as drug addiction.
22. *Laboratories* are research and development centers for disease prevention as well as diagnosis help centers, and so on.
23. *Shamans and traditional medicine* are health care providers based on local wisdom that is still widely used by the community.

Of the 23 institutions listed above that play a role in public health services, the hospital is the most recent, as well as the one most in need of funds. In hospitals, there are expensive, advanced technology and experts from various fields gathered in one place to give the best curative services. Some poor countries even spend more than half their national health budgets to manage their hospitals (WHO, 2001: 13).

Hospital Cost Savings

In line with this, it makes sense that the cost savings of hospitals will have a greater impact than the cost savings from other actors in the health network in a country. In addition, it is very important to study hospital economics to solve economic issues that focus on the hospital and create effects as optimally as possible for universal public health, either directly or indirectly through other institutions in the health care system (Newbrander et al., 1992: 2).

Thus, efforts are being made to save on hospital costs. In the United States in 1989, it is estimated that there was up to 40% waste in health budgets for hospitals. Small improvements in the hospital management system in Malawi were able to produce savings of up to 44% in the budget of the hospital (Newbrander et al., 1992: 2). In Indonesia, a large budget is given to hospitals, but no matter how much is given, it will all run out (Kompas, July 6, 2015).

Ratio of Hospital Beds

Our look at hospital economics is not complete until we look at the ratio of hospital beds to the population. This ratio reflects the number of hospital beds per thousand people. Indeed, there is no global norm for the density standard of hospital beds to the population, but in the countries in Europe, there are 6.3 beds per 1000 people.

The government itself suggests the ideal ratio is two beds per thousand people (1:500) (Table 1.1). The countries with the highest number of beds for 1000 people are Belarus, Japan, and South Korea, with 11.3, 14, and 13.2 beds in 2009. Meanwhile, in the same year, Indonesia had only 0.9 beds per thousand people (WHO, 2009). Data from the Ministry of Health are even lower, namely 0.690 beds per 1000 people.

Table 1.1   Beds per 1000 People in 2009 and 2013

Type of Hospital	Year	Total Hospital	Beds	Beds per 1000 People
Public Hospital	2009	1202	141,603	594
	2013	1725	245,340	987
Private Hospital	2009	321	22,877	96
	2013	503	33,110	133
Total	2009	1523	164,480	690
	2013	2228	278,450	1121
Total population in 2009 was 238,306,561, while in 2013, it was 248,456,215.				

Source: Ministry of Health. 2014. Ministry of Health's Strategic Plan 2015–2019.

In 2013, this ratio increased to 1.121 per 1000. This amount is nonetheless still considered less than the ideal ratio.

In terms of any service preparedness, the hospitals in Indonesia still have many problems. Data in 2011 show that hospital patient admissions per 10,000 people is only 1.9%, with a bed occupancy rate of only 65%. Comprehensive emergency obstetric care of hospitals in districts/cities has reached 25%, while in government hospitals, it reached only 86%. Hospital blood transfusion capability is still low, with an average readiness of 55%, based mainly on the adequacy of new blood supplies by 41% in government hospitals and 13% for private hospitals (Ministry of Health, 2014: 18).

On the other hand, there are still many private hospitals that are reluctant to join the BPJS for economic reasons (Tribune News, September 30, 2014). In fact, 53% of all hospitals in Indonesia are private property (Ministry of Health, 2014: 17). If the economy is used as an excuse, of course we can ask what kind of economic considerations make hospitals decide they lose if they participate in the BPJS. This in turn becomes a topic for the field of hospital economics. Moreover, the benefits gained will allow BPJS to achieve universal coverage and be served by hospitals as a whole without looking again at the possibility of loss. In a more comprehensive manner, the targets to be achieved are efficiency, equity, and sufficient profit for hospitals.

Hospital Economics Issues

Let's start considering the economic issues of hospitals by examining resource issues. A resource issue in hospitals creates many problems, such as an excessive number of patients, poor service quality, lack of diagnostic tools and equipment, dirty and worn-out facilities, long queues at the outpatient clinic, lack of drugs and other medical supplies, low employee morale, and so on (Newbrander et al., 1992: 5).

Newbrander et al. mention three main resource issues in a hospital. These problems are (1992: 5–6):

1. *Resource allocation issues.* This includes resource distribution within the hospital as well as the distribution of the hospital itself in serving patients by type of hospital, territories, communities (urban and rural), vulnerability of the community, and economic wealth of the community (rich and poor). The main economic concepts in this problem are production and cost function. These two functions are related to issues of equality and effectiveness of the hospital. Chapters 3–7 specifically discuss aspects of hospital resource allocation by highlighting productivity, competitiveness, cost components, the economic burden of disease, and economic aspects of infectious diseases originating from the hospital.
2. *Resource management issues.* This issue is related to the use of existing resources in terms of input and output. The main important economic concept is efficiency, including technical efficiency, economical efficiency, and scale, as well as the relationships among these concepts. Chapters 9–12 discuss resource management issues in more detail by highlighting the economic scale, human resource development, quality development, and lean implementation.
3. *Generation resource issues.* These include the issue of how the hospital is able to obtain the resources to run operations without having to cover the access of the strata of the community, thus violating the principle of equality. Chapters 14 and 15 will highlight this aspect specifically by discussing the revenue components of hospitals and diagnosis-related groups (DRGs).

We will take three of these areas as the main framework of this book.

References

CDC. 2013. Centers for Disease Control and Prevention. CDC's Office for State, Tribal, Local and Territorial Support, Atlanta, GA. http://www.cdc.gov/stltpublichealth.

Decree of the Minister of Social Affairs of Indonesia No. 50/HUK/2004 Social Institution Standardization and Social Institution Accreditation Guidelines.

Ministry of Health. 2014. Ministry of Health's Strategic Plan Years 2015–2019.

Kompas. 2015. Health Budget Increases, July 6. http://health.kompas.com/read/2015/07/06/170700723/Anggaran.Kesehatan.Naik.

Newbrander, W., H. Barnum, and J. Kutzin. 1992. *Hospital Economics and Financing in Developing Countries*, Geneva: World Health Organization.

Tribun News. 2014. Kementerian Kesehatan Minta Pemerintah Tambah Anggaran Program. http://www.tribunnews.com/nasional/2014/09/30/kementerian-kesehatan-minta-pemerintah-tambah-anggaran-program-bpjs. (Accessed December 5, 2017.)

WHO. 2001. The Role of Civil Society in Health. Discussion Paper No. 1.

WHO. 2006. The Role of Government in Health Development.

WHO. 2009. World Health Statistics.

Chapter 2

Hospital Resource Allocation

Introduction

The hospital resource allocation issue is concerned with how the government or private hospital owners allocate the budget and other resources in order to achieve maximum results while encouraging equality. The government should consider whether to prioritize a hospital or other health sector, or even other sectors. Furthermore, governments or private institutions, if they have multiple hospitals, have to consider how to allocate the funds to the hospital that they think is the most in need.

Generally, resource allocation to hospitals is done based on the total number of beds available. This is reasonable because the target indicator to be achieved is the ideal ratio of the total number of beds to the population. Even so, another basis may be used, for example the basis of the bed occupancy rate or patient satisfaction (Galal, 2003: 20). Regulation of resource allocation to the hospital can also be rooted in the type of existing health care system.

Resource allocation to hospitals in turn brings different motivations for implementing diagnosis-related groups (DRGs) and how the implementation is executed (Schmid et al., 2010: 465). There are different models of DRGs applied in various countries. A DRG is a disease classification system that later became the basis of payments for hospital care based on recovery, not based on medical and nonmedical services. DRGs are still in the early stages in Indonesia (Rivany, 2009) and only began to develop after the BPJS scheme was present.

Related to the economic aspects of hospital resource allocation, two concepts need to be understood: the production function and the cost.

Production Function

The production function is a mathematical relationship between the output, quantity, and input combinations required to produce (Newbrander et al., 1992: 11). Output is usually viewed as a weighted case mix, while input is usually in the form of items such as the total number of hospital beds; total number of medical staff; and amount of supply, maintenance, and housekeeping.

For example, if the government estimates that there will be 100 nurses graduating from nursing school, then the government should allocate 100 nurses at the existing health centers and hospitals. The aim is to allocate 100 nurses so that the output obtained from this action is the maximum output of the many options for distributing 100 nurses.

For example, the optimal solution is to allocate 40 nurses to hospitals and 60 nurses to community health centers (Newbrander et al., 1992: 8). This means that after 99 nurses are distributed (40 to hospitals and 59 to community health centers), an additional nurse to the hospital, who becomes the 41st nurse, will produce less output than if the nurse became the 60th nurse in the community health centers.

Certainly, it will be more rational to send nurses to the clinic than to the hospital. If the optimal solution is reached, the allocation is said to have achieved allocative efficiency. The point is how the allocation produces the biggest total output.

A hospital production function can be used to examine the effect of particular inputs to hospital production and the differences caused by certain categories, such as the hospital type. Examples of the use of the production function can be seen from the study of Jensen and Morrisey (1986) as follows. In their research, the production function is used to determine the output of the hospital with the allocation of the number of doctors. Output is denoted by Q, adjusted based on case mix. Meanwhile, the input uses the number of doctors L and capital K. The hospitals are free to choose K but not free to choose L directly, but must choose the size of the medical staff S. The number of doctors will depend on the proportion of doctors on the staff (λ). In turn, the proportion size depends on the capital K, which is the input to the doctor and market conditions N, which may be either availability or other hospital appeal. Therefore, mathematically, the production function is formulated as:

$$Q = F(K, L)$$
$$L = \lambda(K, N) \cdot S$$

If both of these equations are differentiated, the following will be obtained:

$$\frac{\partial Q}{\partial K} = \frac{\partial F}{\partial K} + \left(\frac{\partial F}{\partial L}\right) \cdot \left(\frac{\partial \lambda}{\partial K}\right) \cdot S$$

$$\frac{\partial Q}{\partial S} = \left(\frac{\partial F}{\partial L}\right) \cdot \lambda(K, N)$$

From the equation above, if K is increased, it will have two effects on the output Q: first, a direct effect on $\partial F/\partial K$ and second, indirect effects on $(\partial F/\partial L) \cdot (\partial \lambda/\partial K) \cdot S$. This indirect effect works through its ability to attract physicians who are applying for work. Meanwhile, if S is increased, the resulting effect will depend on λ, whose value is less than 1.

Operationally, researchers often use the translog production function. It is often chosen because the form of this function is more flexible so as to allow estimation of the function in fully capturing the possible effects from an input (Jensen and Morrisey, 1986: 432). The translog production function is formulated as follows:

$$\log Q = \beta_0 + \sum_{i=1}^{n} \beta_i (\log X_i) + \sum_{i=1}^{n} \gamma_i (\log X_i)^2$$

$$+ \sum_{i=1}^{n} \sum_{j=1}^{n} \delta_{ij} (\log X_i)(\log X_j) + U$$

with Q as the hospital's output, adjusted to case mix; X_1 to X_n are variables that measure K, S, and N. U is the random disturbance that is assumed to be identical and independently distributed in hospitals.

The first ordo condition (first sigma parts, without squares) of the equation cannot be fulfilled because of managerial errors due to inertia or imperfect information about output requests and input prices. Two of these can be seen as interference with the first ordo equations. If the first ordo equations are combined with the translog basic equations, then the nature of the equation system is a recursive system of a simultaneous block, which can be approximated by the least-squares method, assuming U is not correlated with managerial errors and imperfect information, because these two things are not dependent on hospital control.

Variable translation in the equation can then depend on the situation. The variable Q as the hospital's output variable will vary because the hospital's output can be so many different things. In fact, in a teaching hospital, the output can be health and education output. Typically, the output is calculated using the sum of weighted case types. The weight itself reflects the average cost in taking care of a case. In a study by Jensen and Morrisey, the output is approximated by the number of annual cases handled and the number of annual cases adjusted to case mix. Meanwhile, as the input, the number of medical staff, full-time equivalents (FTEs) from the nursing staff, FTEs of medical residents (especially in a teaching hospital), FTEs of other nondoctor staff, membership in a teaching hospital association (especially in a teaching hospital), and hospital beds, as well as the attendance index of rival hospitals calculated by the ratio of hospital beds to the total hospital beds in the region, are used. A dummy variable in the form of ownership of the hospital and working area of the hospital is also created.

To test the feasibility of the production function, the value of the marginal product is used. The value of the marginal product reflects the contribution of each of the input variable units to the outputs, for example, contribution of a doctor or nurse to the total output. A decent production function should have positive marginal product values for each input to contribute to the output. The equation marginal product MP for hospital i is:

$$MP_i = \sigma_i \cdot \left(\frac{Q}{X_i} \right)$$

with the output elasticity of σ_i for X_i:

$$\sigma_i = \beta_i + 2\gamma_i (\log X_i) + \sum_{\substack{j=1 \\ j \neq 1}}^{n} \delta_{ij} (\log X_j)$$

Further developments produce the data envelopment analysis (DEA) method, which allows a function with a number of double outputs that can be calculated simultaneously with the number of double inputs, too (Banker, 1984). Theory and applications of DEA can be studied further in advanced econometrics texts.

Cost Function

The cost function deals with the relationship between hospital costs and the output level. So, the input in the cost function is not the resource in general, as in the production function, but the financial value from an input. The cost function has an advantage because it can be used to estimate the relationship between the cost and size. This relationship is referred to as the economy of scale, measured by returns to scale. If the input increase is proportional and the output increases steadily, the economy of scale is said to be fixed.

For example, if the amount of doctor working time, nurse working time, supplies, equipment, and beds is increased by 10% and the patients who have been treated increased by 10%, it means that there is a return to a fixed scale. The scale is said to have diseconomies if the increase in size actually reduces output. This could be due to the increasing coordination load and control when input is added. Therefore, it cannot be said directly that the larger the hospital, the better it is. There is an optimum point of hospital size. The closer we get to this point, the greater the return to scale. Once we pass this point, the return to scale will decrease due to increasing operational costs. In the example shown in Figure 2.1, the optimal size is S_0 because at this point, the operating costs are lowest. The operational costs alone are usually operationalized in the hospital long-run average cost (LRAC) (Newbrander et al., 1992: 9).

Decision making solely based on LRAC is certainly incomplete. Operational costs look only at hospital costs and do not consider patient and social costs. These costs need to

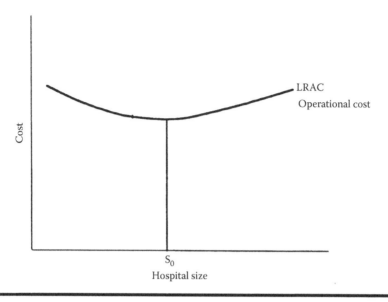

Figure 2.1   Operational cost curve viewed from cost and hospital size.

be considered depending on the distribution of the community. For example, the LRAC estimate concludes that the most optimal bed size is based on the cost incurred by the hospital, which is 200 beds. It is S_0. But when considering the patient costs (e.g., travel costs) and social costs (comfort, closeness to the community), 200 is not optimal. The optimal amount is 150 beds (S_M) (Newbrander et al., 1992: 10) (Figure 2.2).

The decision based on the average cost function alone is still not sufficient in terms of the potential impact if hospitals with high average profits today can potentially experience decreasing marginal benefits if the size is expanded. For example, if there are two hospitals, A and B, A has an average cost of $150 per patient, while B has an average cost of $175. The government can decide to give allocations to A. However, a lower average cost per patient for A might mean that it is on the right of the optimum point, which means it has passed the optimum point. In fact, the addition will lower the average of patient cost further because the marginal cost of each additional patient is greater than the cost of the average

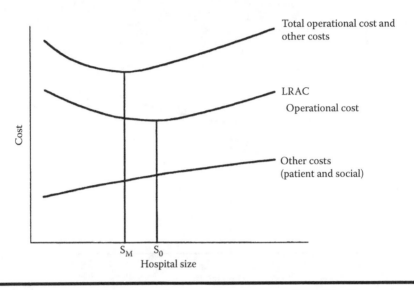

Figure 2.2   Consideration of comprehensive cost function for determination of hospital size.

patient. Meanwhile, hospital B can operate in conditions under which the marginal cost of each additional patient day is less than the average cost of all patients. That is, to make it more capable of being used as a source of decisions, changes in the relative output should be compared with changes in input, rather than just looking at them once.

Generally, the cost function is considered superior to the production function in determining allocation because it uses input prices that are independent of the error rate in the regression equation. Indeed, the issue in the use of the cost function is that it requires input in the form of a price. Several input variables of the hospital are often difficult to estimate in terms of price, for example, the price of medical staff. To overcome this, researchers often regard the number of staff as a constant variable. But this is certainly not realistic because the number of hospital staff tends to change over time. There will be staff who leave (dismissal, retirement, death), and there will be new staff entering (Jensen and Morrisey, 1986: 434).

References

Banker, R. D. 1984. Estimating most productive scale size using data envelopment analysis. *European Journal of Operational Research* 17(1), 35–44.

Galal, A. 2003. *Social Expenditure and the Poor in Egypt.* Egyptian Center for Economic Studies (ECES), Cairo, October 19–20, 2003.

Jensen, G. A. and M. A. Morrisey. 1986. The role of physicians in hospital production. *Review of Economics and Statistics* 68, 432–442.

Newbrander, W., H. Barnum, and J. Kutzin. 1992. *Hospital Economics and Financing in Developing Countries*, Geneva: World Health Organization.

Rivany, R. 2009. Indonesia diagnosis-related groups. *Kesmas Jurnal Kesehatan Masyarakat Nasional* 4(1), 3–9.

Schmid, A. et al. 2010. Explaining health care system change: Problem pressure and the emergence of "hybrid" health care systems. *Journal of Health Politics, Policy and Law* 35(4), 465.

Chapter 3

Hospital Productivity

Introduction

In addition to the cost function, the production function is another hospital resource allocation element. Hospital productivity is a measure of efficiency, which is the total ratio of hospital output produced based on total workforce to total input (workforce, capital, and intermediaries) used to produce this output. Mathematically, hospital productivity is formulated by (Aragon et al., 2017: 2):

$$\text{Productivity} = \frac{\text{Output}}{\text{Input}}$$

There are many types of hospital outputs. Table 3.1 shows various output types depending on the hospital background in detail.

Based on the above-mentioned types of output, hospital outputs that have been weighted as X cost are formulated as follows:

$$X = \sum_{j=1}^{j} (x_j \bar{c_j})$$

Table 3.1 Types of Hospital Outputs

Hospital Background	Output (n)	Unit
Emergency, including ambulance service	Emergency department, minor injury department, special emergency	Attendance, call, patients, incidents
Chemo/radiotherapy and high-priced medicines	Chemotherapy and radiotherapy sessions, high-priced medicines	Treatment cycles, services, attendance, fractions, prescriptions
Community mental health	Pediatric and teenager mental health services, medicine and alcoholic services, specialist health services (e.g., autistic spectrum disorder and eating disorder services), and maintained mental health services (psychiatric hospitals)	Length-of-stay, assessment, cluster days, patient days, contacts, attendance
Community service	Nurse services and health visits for regular and specialist services out of hospital (e.g., patient's house, community health center, etc.), including services provided in certain areas in the broader community (including on a hospital basis if necessary) like midwives, neighborhood health centers, podiatry (reflexology), speech therapy, etc.	Contact, Indonesian Case Base Groups (INA-CBGs) code, attendance, visits, vaccinations
Diagnostic tests	Direct access to diagnostic and pathology services performed on inpatients, critical care patients, outpatients or emergency treatments	Tests

(Continued)

Table 3.1 (Continued)   Types of Hospital Outputs

Hospital Background	Output (n)	Unit
Hospital/patient transport schemes	Financial aid for patients who need to pay travel expenses to and from health service center	Attendance is divided into inpatient, outpatient services, and others
Inpatients	Elective, daily case, and nonelective (emergency stay and maternity)	INA-CBG code
Other health service activities	Audiologist services, hospital in home, daily service facilities, regular day and night stays	Attendance, services provided, scanning, contacts, refinements, patient days, admissions
Outpatients	Visits due to consultation and nonconsultation in clinic at hospital, community health center, common practice, or other locations; Outpatient activity by separated report procedure	Procedures, attendance (face to face or without face to face, single or multiple profession, first or following attendance), INA-CBG code
Radiology	Diagnostic imaging	Examinations
Rehabilitation	Rehabilitation services	Bed days, attendance
Renal dialysis	Renal dialysis, both renal and peritoneal dialysis	Sessions
Specialist services	Specialist palliative services, cystic fibrosis, critical care services, coroner care installation, cancer interdisciplinary teams	Bed days, attendance, patient travel, long travel, patients, care planning

Source: Aragon, M. J. A. et al. 2017. *Hospital Trusts Productivity in the English NHS: Uncovering Possible Drivers of Productivity Variations.* University of York, Centre for Health Economics.

where x_j is the number of patients categorized in the output category of j with $j = 1, \ldots, J$ in a hospital; and c_j is the cost weight, which is formulated as:

$$\bar{c}_j = \frac{c_j}{\hat{c}}$$

where c_j is the national average cost for patients allocated on j, and the c outputs are the national average cost of all patients (Aragon et al., 2017).

Meanwhile, for input, employment, capital, and intermediary input indicators can be used. Intermediary capital and input are distinguished based on time. Capital is all nonworkforce inputs with asset ages of more than a year. Land and buildings are examples of capital. Intermediary input has an asset age of less than a year.

These three types of input are combined into one formula:

$$Z^{TF} = Z^{L} + E^{M} + E^{K}$$

where Z^{TF} is hospital output, Z^{L} is employment input, E^{M} is intermediary goods and services, and E^{K} is capital. Employment input is calculated with the formula:

$$Z^{L} = Z^{DL} + E^{A}$$

where Z^{DL} is the direct employment input, and E^{A} is the hospital staff expense. E^{A} can be replaced by the quantity of staff employed by the hospital. Z^{DL} is calculated by the equation:

$$Z^{DL} = \sum_{n=1}^{N} Z_n \omega_n$$

where Z_n is the input type volume with $n = 1, \ldots, N$; and ω_n is the national average wage for n type input (Aragon et al., 2017: 3).

Meanwhile, total factor productivity is formulated as:

$$P^L = \frac{X}{Z^L} + \frac{\sum_{j=1}^{J} X_j \overline{C_j}}{\sum_{n=1}^{N} Z_n \omega_n + E^A + E^M + E^K}$$

If the productivity is going to be tested on a certain level (for instance, nationally), then the productivity needs to be standardized to be more easily interpreted and compared. Workforce productivity and total factor standardizations are performed by comparing them to national totals, then formed into percentages through:

$$P_h^{S,L} = \left\{ \left[\left(\frac{X_h}{Z_h^L} \right) \middle/ \left(\frac{1}{H} \sum_h \frac{X_h}{Z_h^L} \right) \right] - 1 \right\} \times 100$$

$$P_h^{S,TF} = \left\{ \left[\left(\frac{X_h}{Z_h^L} \right) \middle/ \left(\frac{1}{H} \sum_h \frac{X_h}{Z_h^{TF}} \right) \right] - 1 \right\} \times 100$$

where the h index indicates the individual hospital, so $P_h^{S,L}$ is the standard workforce for hospital h; X_h is hospital output h, and so on. Meanwhile, H is the total number of national hospitals. The obtained amount indicates the hospital productivity level h against the national average. For instance, if $P_h^{S,L}$ is 10, then hospital h has workforce productivity of 10% above the national average.

Hospital Productivity Factors

To examine factors affecting productivity, the linear equation principle is applied. Generally, it is known that hospital productivity is affected by four factors (Aragon et al., 2017: 4):

1. *Hospital characteristics.* Some hospital characteristics that
   need to be considered include the following.
   a. Ratio of the number of students to the number of medi-
      cal and nonmedical workforce. This ratio applies to
      teaching hospitals that double as educational centers.
      Teaching hospitals generally have higher costs than
      nonteaching hospitals because they use funds not only
      for patient care but also for medical student teaching
      and other health services. This hospital is also less pro-
      ductive compared to nonteaching hospitals because it
      tends to treat more complex or chronic patients. Doctors
      also have a double role. In addition to being health
      care officers, they are also lecturers who train medical
      students. If a hospital is not a teaching one, then this
      indicator is 0. The use of the student ratio is better than
      a dummy variable alone to signify a teaching hospital
      identity because the more students, the harder it is to
      provide productive care. The student ratio gives a weak
      positive effect toward hospital workforce productivity
      and even gives a negative effect toward hospital total
      productivity, although it is categorized as weak.
   b. *Ownership.* Hospitals can be different based on their
      ownership: private or public, regional public service
      agency or not, and so on. Generally, private hospitals
      are more productive than public, especially in terms of
      total productivity.
   c. *Size.* The size of a hospital is generally examined
      based on the number of beds (Aiken et al., 2014) or
      the mortality level (Propper et al., 2004). The more
      beds, the higher the complexity, and this may cause a
      decrease of productivity.
   d. *Medical workforce ratio to overall workforce.* Generally,
      a huge medical workforce ratio can increase workforce
      productivity significantly. However, this also decreases
      total productivity due to the large consumption of
      resources.

e. *Market strength factor.* This indicator indicates the inevitable geographical differences in hospitals. The market strength factor is calculated based on staff index; medical and dental weight, capital city; buildings, lands, and others (all unchanged indicators based on location) (Monitor, 2013). In certain areas, staff costs (nonmedical, medical, dental), land, and buildings can be far more expensive than in other places; hence, they have high market strength factors. The higher the market strength, the lower the productivity.

2. *Service quality.* A common indicator used for exact hospital service quality is patient survival level in the 30 days after being discharged from the hospital. This indicator obtains patient immortality in the hospital or 30 days after being discharged from the hospital. The formula for the patient survival level is in the form of a percentage below:

$$\left(1 - \frac{\text{Immortality in hospital or in 30 days after discharge}}{\text{Total length of stay}}\right) \times 100$$

The higher the patient survival level, the higher the workforce productivity because there is a spirit that comes from success in taking care of patients. However, high patient survival reduces total productivity instead because there are many costs to be paid to bring about a high patient survival level. This means the more qualified the service, the more resources are expended to provide the service, therefore reducing total productivity.

3. *Patient characteristics.* A patient characteristic that has been found to strongly relate to productivity is patient age. The examination of this characteristic is conducted by dividing patients' bed days by the relevant group of age by total bed days of all patients, multiplied by 100. There are four patient age groups that affect hospital productivity.

    a. *Patients in the last year of life.* The more patients who are in the last year of their lives, the higher the hospital productivity. This is actually inappropriate because it reflects that hospitals tend to neglect patients in the last year of life and dedicate more resources to patients with longer life spans. However, there is also the so-called red herring hypothesis stating that the highest health service cost is for elderly patients.

    b. *Patients 0–15 years old.* The more neonate, infant, child, or teenager patients, the lower the hospital productivity. This is due to the hardship of taking care of patients in this age group.

    c. *Patients 46–60 years old.* Similar to young patients, older patients give hospitals productivity problems as well because of medical condition complexity that needs many resources.

    d. *Patients above 60 years old.* Elderly patients reduce hospital productivity as well because patients in this group tend to experience sickness complications and are hard to cure.

      As can be seen, patients 16–45 years old do not affect hospital productivity. This is because this age group is very heterogeneous, and people within it have various types of medical conditions, from mild to severe. Meanwhile, the very young age group (babies, children, teenagers), adults (older adults), and very old (elderly) have more complex disease homogeneity than those in middle age.

4. *Resource use efficiency.* Resource use efficiency is generally calculated by the following two indicators.

    a. *Daily case and elective stay ratio.* The more daily cases, the lower the hospital productivity.

    b. *Average length of stay (ALOS).* The higher patients' length of stay, the more hospital productivity tends to decrease because patients with long stays cost more and tend to have complex diseases.

References

Aiken, L. H., Sloane, D. M., Bruyneel, L., Van den Heede, K., Griffiths, P., Busse, R. et al. 2014. Nurse staffing and education and hospital mortality in nine European countries: A retrospective observational study. *Lancet* 383(9931), 1824–1830.

Aragon, M. J. A., Castelli, A., and Gaughan, J. 2017. Hospital trusts productivity in the English NHS: Uncovering possible drivers of productivity variations. *PLoS ONE* 12(8), e0182253. https://doi.org/10.1371/journal.pone.0182253.

Monitor, 2013. *A Guide to the Market Forces Factor.* NHS England Publications Gateway.

Propper, C., Burgess, S., and Green, K. 2004. Does competition between hospitals improve the quality of care? Hospital death rates and the NHS internal market. *Journal of Public Economics* 88, 1247–1272.

Chapter 4

Hospital Competition and Quality

Introduction

We may think that the greater the competition, the higher the hospital quality because each hospital competes to provide the best service to attract customers. However, this does not apply to the hospital market generally. Some relationships may be negative depending on how we measure the quality as well as how big the market and capital city factor are. The same issue occurs in the relationship between competition and patient satisfaction. For instance, if a hospital deals with competition through nonethical means, this kind of competition produces poor-quality service as well as patient dissatisfaction.

Competition versus Quality

The assumption that the greater the hospital competition, the higher the quality comes from a view that hospitals run for the same price. In this situation, a hospital is able to increase competitiveness only by increasing quality (because increasing

or decreasing prices cannot be done). The greater the competition, the more responsive the demand for quality, because
patients will evaluate a hospital based on its quality to obtain
more benefits for the same price. In line with this, a hospital
that increases its quality will attract more patients and, hence,
obtain a larger income; if a hospital tries to maximize the profit
it makes from the market and the marginal price for adding patients is fixed as well, a hospital always meets patients'
demands, which is the basis of quality expectation. This brings
on an increase of the profit margin, which is the difference
between the marginal price and the cost of additional patients.

An increase in competition can decrease quality as well.
The source is the profit margin. If the profit margin is negative, the hospital will take a loss if increasing its quality. As a
result, hospitals consider lowering quality up to a minimum
point as far as not breaking requirements, such as quality
minimum requirements as set by the government, and not
incurring any malpractice claims by patients. The profit margin
may be low if one of these events occurs:

1. *The marginal cost proportion against the cost is high.* As
   a result, adding one patient with high-quality treatment
   will be costly, even more so if patients are multiplying. If
   the cost stays high and the marginal cost is low, the cost
   of adding a patient will be covered by patients' bills. This
   means a hospital with a small amount of capital will find
   it hard to attract patients without decreasing its quality.
   A hospital with a large amount of capital will be able to
   attract a high number of patients because the cost to add
   patients is low due to its having a high fixed cost.
2. *Marginal cost increases.* The more patients a hospital
   adds, the higher the marginal cost, so it cannot be covered by patients. In line with this, hospitals with fixed or
   lower marginal costs will obtain a positive profit margin.
3. *Service costs do not include investment/capital cost.* In this
   situation, no one pays for hospital investment/capital and

the hospital eventually experiences loss. On the contrary, if the service cost includes investment/capital cost as well, then the profit margin is larger.

Nonfinancial Factors

There are also some nonfinancial factors affecting the relationship between hospital competition and service quality. These factors include:

1. *Altruism (kindness) of health providers.* A hospital is ready to treat patients who are not advantageous to the hospital or patients who have a negative profit margin. The hospital is able to perform this because in addition to being profit oriented, it is also community health oriented. Some hospitals can act altruistically, which is prioritizing patients' benefit rather than the hospital's. This is especially true of good doctors who are motivated to cure patients without considering the cost and who will pay the bill. If the strength of such an altruist doctor is greater than the influence of managers (who only care about obstacles and financial targets), then the hospital's quality will be lower due to the depletion of resources to cure patients who do not pay. However, this negative effect is balanced by hospital attraction. A good hospital will attract more patients, and this will optimize fixed cost, for example, maximizing the use of equipment and not having idle nurses. So, the result of the cost and benefit for the hospital from competition depends on which will win: either the higher marginal cost because patients do not pay or the more efficient fixed cost because many patients are treated.

2. *The release of quality information to patients.* Patients or doctors will spend some cost to compare the available hospital service quality. If the hospital provides accurate quality information, patients are sure that they are

in the correct hospital compared to those that do not provide data. A hospital that provides quality data can be assumed to be better than those that do not, which are assumed to be covering some bad qualities. However, hospital demands depend on the difference in patient errors in monitoring hospital quality (rating them as too good or too bad), not just on quality differences among hospitals. If quality differences among hospitals are great and the level of patient error in monitoring hospital quality is high, then the profit margin will be high for those increasing quality as well. However, in reality, patients are more careful in evaluating hospitals, so the level of mistakes is commonly low. If the level of errors is low and the quality difference among hospitals is large, then the range of patients attracted will be low. Information provision on hospital quality to patients will decrease patients' evaluation error level instead and focus patients on each individual hospital, causing marginal cost to increase quality. This situation generates consequences if hospital quality information provision has a positive effect on profit margin only if the quality difference among hospitals is not so great. However, if the case is brought to general practitioners who are paid by a capitation system (cost per person), then they have to compete and provide quality information. Competition will increase the number of patients and increase profit for the same cost per capita. However, if competition takes place but doctors do not provide quality information and patients are confronted with low-quality information, that decreases the effectiveness of general practitioners' service quality against the amount of capitation.

3. *The role of drugstores, clinics, class C hospitals, community health centers, and other gatekeepers.* Gatekeepers are primary health service centers related to hospitals through a referral system. In the BPJS system, a patient should first go to this primary service, and if he or she cannot be

cured, he or she is referred to the hospital. The role of the primary health service in significant competition is that all patients who need to go to the hospital should be referred from this center. If the primary health service's quality in diagnosing patients' symptoms is high, then the primary service center will act to suppress competition because it will refer patients to a clear specialist. However, if the primary health service's diagnosis quality is low, this center does not have a clear destination to which it should refer the patients. As a result, there are many choices for referral, and these choices may cause a more even spread, leading to larger competition.

4. *"Cream skim" and "skimp."* Cream skim is hospital behavior that increases service quality to beneficial patients (wealthy and royal); meanwhile, skimp is the opposite hospital behavior, decreasing service quality to harmful or less beneficial patients. These two behaviors break health service equality principles, although they do occur in the field. This behavior increases along with a competition increase because hospitals are eager to attract as many beneficial patients as possible so the patients do not move to competitor hospitals, and to refuse harmful patients wherever possible so the patients go to a competitor hospital.

5. *Cost caging.* If the cost cannot be changed by the hospital, the hospital has no other choice than to tighten its budget. The aim to reduce cost will result in profit from cost reduction similar to business marginal disutility. This minimizing effort can be interpreted as minimizing as much cost as possible to reach a position in which utility reaches a lower point, after which the quality will decrease. For example, if electrical expenses can be maintained, this cost should be minimized up to reaching a minimum point. Indeed, this minimum point does not mean turning off power, but maintaining the power to be used for necessities so that it does not make patients

conclude that service quality at the hospital is bad (due to lack of light). If saving means a quality increase, cost saving (caging) will be huge because marginal profit will be achieved through the mass adding of patients. On the contrary, if saving means a quality decrease, hospitals tend to decrease saving and further decrease it with a competition increase.

6. *Wait time.* Competition among hospitals is controlled by wait time in addition to quality. If the number of patients in a hospital is too high, there will be wait time, and this naturally encourages patients to move to another hospital. Because the number of visits to a hospital depends on many factors, one of which is quality, the risk of visiting a less busy hospital is lower quality. Patients should eventually choose either waiting in a long line to obtain high-quality service or waiting in a short one to obtain a low quality of service. The higher the level of competition, the lower the wait time because there are many hospitals among which patients can choose. On the other hand, a long wait time will encourage competition because other hospitals will see more opportunity to attract patients looking for a short wait time.

7. *Competitive area.* The competitive area of a hospital is highly related to geography. One patient selection criterion to get to a hospital is travel mileage, especially in emergency cases. If there are two locations, Regency A and Regency B, and Regency A has two hospitals, hospitals X and Y, while Regency B has hospital Z, the competitor of hospital X is hospital Y, and the competitor of hospital Y is hospital Z, which means that the competitor of hospital Z is hospital X as well. However, hospital Y is the competitor of hospital Z due to the short distance between them, and they compete in attracting patients located between their ranges. Similarly, hospital Y is the competitor of hospital X as well because the distance between the hospitals is short, and they compete to attract patients located

between them. This means hospital Y has two competi-
tors; meanwhile, hospitals X and Z have one competitor
each, which is hospital Y. The competition encountered by
hospital Y is tighter; hence, it should increase its quality so
it can beat hospitals X and Z.

8. *Market size.* In line with the above overview, it is already
clear that market size decides the competition. Market size
is determined by mileage, travel expense, population size,
and patient density. Hospital and patient spatial grouping can be investigated using a special statistical method
developed by Imbens et al. (2011).

9. *Market structure.* Market structure can be in the form of
monopoly, duopoly, oligopoly, or high competition, up to
perfect competition. Market structure is frequently used
as a competition indicator. Market structure is collectively
measured using the Herfindahl–Hirschman index (HHI),
which is the sum of market segments squared and all the
hospitals in one competitive area. At an individual level,
market structure is measured using market segments,
which is the actual number of patients in a hospital
against the number of patients in a competitive area.

10. *Market dynamic* (Brekke et al., 2010). There are some
types of quality that have characteristics, like stock. This
quality increases only if investment is higher than the
depreciation rate. In order for investment to have a higher
rate, new investments should be performed so there is
always short-term revision on investment decisions. This
especially occurs along with the rise of competition. This
means the tighter the competition, the more frequently
hospitals need to revise their quality of investment. If a
decrease of investment occurs in a hospital, a competitor
will see it as a sign to gain a profit and, hence, also reduce
its investment rather than increasing it. This means, aggre-
gately, competition will bring about a quality decrease.

11. *Specialization* (Calem and Rizzo, 1995). Specialization, if
seen from an economic perspective, is a way to get out

of competition by creating a new niche. For example, in a city there are six public hospitals. A new hospital will choose to construct a delivery hospital so it does not have a competitor. What will be used as a specialization area will depend on the cost. If there are three specialization areas, such as heart, cancer, and delivery, and the cost for delivery is far higher than the costs for heart and cancer, then the new hospital may choose to construct a delivery hospital. However, if high cost encourages the community to ask for higher quality, then the consideration to construct a delivery hospital needs to be delayed or postponed because the investors need to construct a more expensive delivery hospital (because the profit margin is small) rather than constructing a delivery clinic in a public hospital if the patients do not want to pay a higher cost than the cost of a public hospital.

References

Brekke, K. R., R. Cellini, L. Siciliani, and O. R. Straume. 2010. Competition and quality in health care markets: A differential-game approach. *Journal of Health Economics* 29(4), 508–523.

Calem, P. and J. Rizzo. 1995. Competition and specialization in the hospital industry: An application of Hotelling's location model. *Southern Economic Journal* 61(4), 1182–1198. doi: 10.2307/1060749

Gravelle, H., R. Santos, L. Sicialiani, and R. Goudie. 2012. *Hospital Quality Competition under Fixed Prices*, New York: University of York.

Imbens, G., T. Barrios, R. Diamond, and M. Kolesar. 2011. *Clustering, Spatial Correlations and Randomization Inference*. (Mimeo), Harvard University.

Chapter 5

Cost Components in Medical Procedures

Introduction

All medical procedures in a hospital will contain a cost component. This cost component is present not only for the medical procedure directly, but also from a variety of other activities performed before and after medical procedures are done. Calculation of the cost of medical procedures should be done when dealing with two equally effective medical procedures. If there are two equally effective medical procedures, cost review is necessary to obtain the most cost-effective procedure. This is important because it is associated with a public policy perspective. For the public, the cost they pay for the National Health Insurance (JKN) program should be optimal for the healing of patients. Costs above the optimum would increase the burden on the community that gives donations, and this has the potential to cause many patients to be treated poorly. Costs that are less than optimal would be detrimental to the hospital and provide problems for the hospital's continuity.

Cost Elements

In calculating the costs of components of medical procedures, the costs must be calculated starting from when the patient initiated the diagnosis process. This calculation should be separated between inpatient and outpatient costs, although the cost elements from both types of treatment are the same. In general, the cost elements of a complex medical procedure that involves the use of an operating room include:

1. *Cost of diagnosis.* The cost of diagnosis may vary depending on the disease. Diagnosis can be clinical (based on the symptoms of the disease) or based on specific tests using test procedures involving medical instruments. Most of the costs of diagnosis can involve the use of special instruments such as an electrocardiogram (EKG). Thus, the minimum cost of diagnosis consists of doctors' costs and instrument costs.

2. *Cost of the emergency room.* This cost applies to patients who are dealing with life-threatening emergencies such as heart attack, stroke, and major trauma. Unfortunately, a visit to the emergency room often deals with patients who can be treated in clinics or community health centers. Surveys in the United States showed that 66.7–95.7% of visits to the emergency department are not needed (Weinick et al., 2010). Patients who are not in emergency situations should not be advised to go to the emergency room unless the patient does not have time to wait in other places or has his or her own considerable resources to bear the cost of the emergency room. There are two reasons for this. First, the fixed costs of the emergency room are considered high since it needs to pay the staff to be on standby for 24 hours, 7 days a week, complete with expensive instruments that are able to handle even the most serious cases. Fixed costs must still be paid by

the patient even if the patient suffered minor injuries. As a result, lightly injured patients treated in the emergency have to pay 3.5 times more than patients treated with the same problem in a regular clinic (Weinick et al., 2010). Second, if patients with common problems are left in the emergency room, crowded situations can occur, and patients who really need emergency care have to wait, and their safety will be increasingly threatened. Components of the cost of emergency care are related to salaries, instruments, lab tests, and the cost of transportation by ambulance. Variations in the cost of emergencies are enormous, starting at Rp 50,000 and even going up to Rp 1 billion (Caldwell et al., 2013). It is important in this cost to look at the real cost of emergencies because sometimes the cost of an emergency is deliberately increased to cover losses in other departments in the hospital, so patient billing does not necessarily reflect the real cost of emergency care.

3. *Cost of the laboratory.* Components of the cost of the laboratory depend on the type of test used. The more complex, the greater the costs for lab assignments. The costs charged to patients include salary, materials, instruments, and lab general costs (administration, security, building, care, and pharmacy). General costs are usually the largest component and can reach almost half the cost of the lab. The second-largest component is the cost of materials (Ninci and Ocakacon, 2004). The rest is the cost of instruments (blood banks, microscopes, incubators, centrifuges, photometers, conditioners, mixers, ovens, safety cabinets, autoclaves, washing, etc.) and service costs. For a patient, this cost can be the cumulative cost obtained from a number of lab tests for both clinical and anatomic pathology. The cost of the lab for surgical patients is generally higher than the cost of the lab for medical patients (Young et al., 2000).

4. *Cost of the operating room.* The cost of the operating room includes the cost of anesthesia, the recovery room, and surgery (Mehio et al., 2011). These costs are calculated starting from the patient's admission and include induction of anesthesia, placement, preparation, surgical procedures, transport preparation, discharge, and the recovery room. Approximately 15% of the costs of the operating room come from schedule inefficiencies due to a full recovery room, cancellation of surgery, patients not being ready, cleaning time, or doctors being unavailable (McLaughlin, 2012).

5. *Cost of pharmaceuticals.* The cost of pharmaceuticals includes all costs incurred for medicines. These costs include pharmaceutical costs incurred by emergency, surgery preparation, operating room, surgery, and other drug costs.

6. *Cost of radiology.* Certain imaging services can be quite expensive, while others are cheap. These costs change depending on changes in technology in the field of radiology and related fields. An estimated 38–62% increase in hospital costs from 1940–1990 was caused by changes in radiological technology and other fields (AAFP, 2012). Broadly speaking, the cost of radiology is divided into two components, the cost of labor and nonlabor costs. Labor costs include the costs of management, technicians, nurses, secretaries, receptionists/schedulers, the film librarian, patient callers, maintenance of instruments, information systems, quality assurance, and so on. Nonlabor costs include equipment, drugs, films, medical-surgical supplies, hospital payments, office supplies, linens, and uniforms. Instruments can be in the form of general diagnostic radiography, ultrasonography, computed tomography, magnetic resonance imaging and scintigraphy examination, and interventional radiology (Saini et al., 2000).

7. *Cost of respiratory support.* This cost includes the cost of life support for patients hospitalized in critical condition in the hospital.
8. *Cost of rooms.* The cost of rooms include the costs of basic home supplies (baths, cleaning bedsheets, beds, televisions) and food costs.
9. *Cost of supplies.* The cost of supplies includes medical and surgical supplies, implants, bandages, vaccines, syringes, and other materials other than drugs.
10. *Cost of therapy.* The cost of therapy is associated with patient recovery after medical procedures are performed, outside the cost of pharmaceuticals and others that have been mentioned.
11. *Other costs.* Other costs may include services purchased from vendors outside the hospital (rental, leasing, travel, consulting, etc.) for the benefit of patient recovery. Sometimes, to treat certain diseases, the health care service should receive training, and training costs can be seen as other costs. Also included in other expenses are the costs of amortization and depreciation, risk, and interest if patients delay the payments (Aiena, 2011).

Analysis of Covariance

After all costs for any medical procedure are known, the difference in total hospital costs for medical procedures compared is calculated statistically using analysis of covariance (ANCOVA). However, first, the costs distribution should be examined through the data normality test to determine whether a transformation is needed. Once the data are ascertained as normal, either with or without transformation, then the ANCOVA procedure is executed.

In the ANCOVA procedure, the cost calculation from each element above needs to be adjusted to the patient characteristics. These characteristics are adjusted by taking them into account as covariates in ANCOVA. Patient characteristics generally taken into account in the costs adjustment include, among others:

1. *Patient age.* Patient age has a strong correlation with health status. In modern society, generally, the higher the patient age, the greater or more severe the health problems faced. Studies in Australia on nonindigenous people who can be considered to have a more modern lifestyle than the indigenous people show that health status decreases, with a peak at the age of 74 years. That is, if the patient is older, there is a greater possibility that health problems will occur; therefore, a given medical procedure is more complicated and costly. In traditional communities, the relationship of age with health status tends to be weaker. As shown in the case of Australia, indigenous peoples have the biggest health problems not in old age, but rather between the ages of 50 and 65 (Figure 5.1). The residents who are older have better health status. Thus, it appears there is "a kind of critical point" in the health status of traditional society, that is, at the age of retirement. If people pass this age, the community from the traditional group is even more healthy. We can see this in villages in Indonesia where elderly people who are grandparents look healthier than the middle-aged population. Indeed, several studies in other countries also show that health care costs do not depend on age. There is no significant correlation between age and health in general health (Chong, 2009) and mental health (Blazer and Hybels, 2005). In fact, after the age of 65, there are reports that health costs actually decline, after increasing gradually since adolescence. Meanwhile, there are also reported cases of health care costs decreasing as people get older, with the greatest cost for infants who suffer health problems (Raitano, 2006), so it seems the relationship between

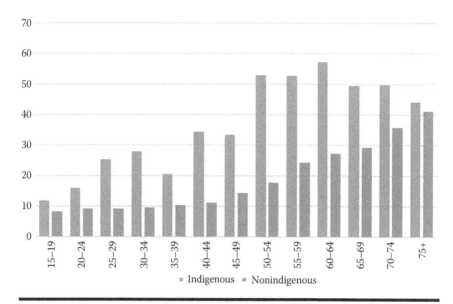

Figure 5.1 Age group percentages with poor health status based on indigenous status in Australia. (Adapted from Gray, M. C. et al. 2002. *Health Expenditure, Income, and Health Status among Indigenous and Other Australians.* **Canberra, Australia: ANU Press, 34.)**

age and health costs is relatively complex. But this gives us something to consider, so we control the age in weighing the health costs in a medical procedure.

2. *Sex of the patient.* In terms of life expectancy, women live longer than men (Figure 5.2). This can be due to lifestyle factors. Women are more likely to contact the hospital when facing health problems than men. Moreover, when women face health problems, they tend to immediately stop the activities that place them at risk, unlike men. As a result, throughout the twentieth century until today, women always live longer than men. Of course, this does not mean that women's health issues are fewer or less serious than those of men. It could be precisely that women's health issues are greater than those of men because women live longer. In fact, women actually have a higher disease rate than men (Helgeson, 2015: 350). Women are more

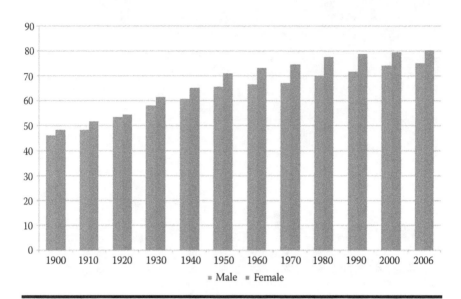

Figure 5.2 Life expectancy in the twentieth century by sex. (Adapted from Helgeson, V. 2015. *Psychology of Gender*. New Jersey: Pearson Education, 344.)

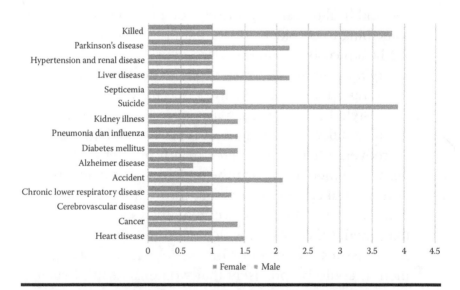

Figure 5.3 Mortality ratio of women and men based on disease causes. (Adapted from Helgeson, V. 2015. *Psychology of Gender*. New Jersey: Pearson Education, 346.)

likely to get diseases than men, but men are more likely to experience severe disease than women (Figure 5.3).

3. *Admission status.* Admission status can be either elective or emergency. Patients with elective status are not in an emergency situation and can be on different care pathways from a patient in emergency status. In line with this, the maintenance costs will also vary between elective and emergency patients.

4. *Severity of illness.* Patients who come through the emergency room, as mentioned earlier, do not necessarily have a high severity of illness. Therefore, the severity of illness should also be considered as a predictor for the cost of medical procedures.

References

AAFP. Family physician interpretation of outpatient radiographs. 2012. http://www.aafp.org/about/policies/all/radiology.html.

Aiena, C. 2011. *Budgeting Basics 101: The Nuts and Bolts of Budget Planning.* Boston: Massachusetts General Hospital.

Blazer, D. G. and C. F. Hybels. 2005. Origins of depression in later life. *Psychological Medicine* 35(9), 1241–1252.

Caldwell, N. et al. 2013. How much will I get charged for this? Patient charges for top ten diagnoses in the emergency department. *PloS One* 8(2), e55491.

Chong, W. D. 2009. The influence of acculturation, religiosity, and forgiveness style on the general health of Korean Americans. PhD dissertation, Liberty University.

Gray, M. C., B. H. Hunter, and J. Taylor. 2002. *Health Expenditure, Income, and Health Status among Indigenous and Other Australians.* Canberra, Australia: ANU Press.

Helgeson, V. 2015. *Psychology of Gender.* New Jersey: Pearson Education.

McLaughlin, M. M. 2012. A Model to Evaluate Efficiency in Operating Room Processes. PhD dissertation, University of Michigan.

Mehio, A. K. et al. 2011. Comparative hospital economics and patient presentation: Vertebroplasty and kyphoplasty for the treatment of vertebral compression fracture. *American Journal of Neuroradiology*, 32.7, 1290–1294.

Ninci, A., and R. Ocakacon. 2004. How much do lab tests cost? Analysis of Lacor Hospital laboratory services. *Health Policy and Development*, 2(2), 144–150.

Raitano, M. 2006. *The Impact of Death-Related Costs on Health-Care Expenditure: A Survey*. ENEPRI Research Report No. 17.

Saini, S. et al. 2000. Technical cost of radiologic examinations: Analysis across imaging modalities 1. *Radiology*, 216.1, 269–272.

Weinick, R. M., R. M. Burns, and A. Mehrotra. 2010. Many emergency department visits could be managed at urgent care centers and retail clinics. *Health Affairs*, 29.9, 1630–1636.

Young, D. S., B. S. Sachais, and L. C. Jefferies. 2000. Laboratory costs in the context of disease. *Clinical Chemistry*, 46.7, 967–975.

Chapter 6

Economic Burden
of Disease

Introduction

The issue of the economic burden of disease is a study that
includes three disciplines: health economics, pharmaceutical
economics, and hospital economics. All three are interrelated.
When speaking from the perspective of hospital economics,
the problem of the economic burden of disease is associated
with the costs of hospital care. The calculation of the economic burden of disease is important because it can help raise
awareness about the severity of an illness, placing the issue
in the context of other public health concerns, and can be
used as an economic evaluation of interventions to reduce or
prevent disease occurrence (Fang et al., 2012: 157).

Perspectives on Study of the Economic Burden

A study of economic burden can use one of two perspectives.
The first is a prevalence-based approach (Fang et al., 2012:
157). A prevalence-based approach calculates the prevalence
of direct and indirect costs for one period, usually one year, as

a result of the prevalence of a disease in the period in question regardless of the time of emergence of the disease in patients. This means it weighs all cases of the disease (including cases with emergence in or at any time prior to the basis year), but only the costs that appear in the one-year period are calculated.

The second approach is incident based. The incident-based approach calculates the total cost of all time generated from new cases of the disease occurring over a period of time, for example, one year. This cost is difficult to measure because it also includes long-term costs and consequences of a disease. This includes, for example, the sequence of chronic health, employment, and income throughout a person's lifespan, but this method is the most effective method to evaluate the economic aspects of disease prevention or intervention activities. With the incident-based approach, we can compare the lifetime costs and prevention costs of one case of disease through analysis of profit and loss prevention.

The incident-based approach is especially suitable for diseases in a group of chronic diseases rather than acute diseases. The acute group includes diseases that emerge suddenly, with signs and symptoms related to the disease process itself; take place in the short term; and have two potential outcomes: recovery and return to the previous activity, or death (Lubkin and Larsen, 2006: 5).

The group of chronic diseases includes diseases that are sustainable indefinitely. These diseases can emerge suddenly or through hidden processes, have exacerbation episodes, or keep running without any symptoms for a long time. The U.S. Commission on Chronic Illness defines chronic diseases as having permanence; residual inabilities; nonpathological changes; and the need for rehabilitation or control, surveillance, and long-term care (Lubkin and Larsen, 2006: 5). Long-term effects or iatrogenic effects of a disease can also be chronic conditions. Some life-saving procedures can provide new problems for the patient's life, such as malabsorption problems due to radiation in the treatment of metastatic colon cancer. While chemotherapy can reduce the problem of cancer, it brings up significant risks of leukemia in the future. The naturally declining quality of a person's health over time in the elderly also means chronic diseases cannot be completely cured. Older patients will require more specialized services due to conditions that are increasingly complex (Lubkin and Larsen, 2006: 5).

The Economic Burden of Disease

The economic burden of disease is divided into two categories, direct costs and indirect costs. Direct costs include all types of costs spent for medical needs. These costs include (Panatto et al., 2015):

1. *Cost of treatment.* Cost of treatment includes all kinds of drug costs such as antiviral, analgesics, anti-epileptics, antidepressants, topical agents, antibiotics, ophthalmo-logical products, nerve blocks, laser treatments, surgical therapy, and other forms of therapeutic appliances.
2. *Cost of medical examinations.* This cost includes the cost of primary care visits, emergency visits, specialist consultations, and other professional visit costs.
3. *Cost of hospitalization and hospital emergencies.*
4. *Cost of diagnostic tests and procedures.* This cost includes costs such as chest and abdominal X-rays, ultrasounds, blood and urine tests, electrocardiograms, and molecular tests.
5. *Cost of other health-related resources.* These costs may include, for example, a transcutaneous electrical nerve stimulator.

Indirect costs are costs incurred due to loss of productivity and patients who do not work. Costs such as these cause problems in patients' careers, mainly because patients need to take temporary leave for treatment. Even if the patients are forced to work, their productivity still decreases. The loss of productivity can also be caused by problems such as pain or discomfort, loss of concentration, and fatigue when working, as well as the side effects of a treatment occurring while working. Total productivity is lost when patients should not work for a number of reasons, such as a recommendation or a medical appointment, fear of the spread of infectious diseases in the workplace so that patients are sent home, or patients undergoing intensive treatment in the hospital. When patients are treated at home, they must also get a private nurse, particularly in cancer patients, so this should also be taken into account in the cost analysis.

Indirect costs are also related to the sociological role of a sufferer of disease. In developing countries, a sick person is required to take a sick role in the community. The sick role is characterized by four things (Lubkin and Larsen, 2006: 24):

1. Individuals break away from normal social roles.
2. Individuals are not responsible for their disease.
3. Individuals are obliged to want to recover from illness.
4. Individuals are obliged to look for and cooperate with competent technical assistance.

Sociological Role

The sociological role in turn becomes the basis for the sick behavior of a person. There are three types of health behaviors (Lubkin and Larsen, 2006: 24):

1. Health behavior consists of actions taken by a person who believes that he/she is healthy, with the aim to prevent disease or detect it in the asymptomatic stage.
2. Sick behavior is any action taken by someone who feels himself/herself to be ill to determine the state of health

and find appropriate healing. This behavior includes the various ways individuals respond to their physical indications, how they oversee their internal circumstances and take recovery actions, and how they use various care resources, both formal and informal.

3. Sick role behavior also includes activities carried out by someone with the aim to recover by those who feel they are ill.

Stigma

Indirect costs that are more difficult to calculate are the costs generated by stigma. A stigma is any social construction related to categories of people based on attributes and characteristics that bring shame or neglect (Lubkin and Larsen, 2006: 48). Most chronic diseases bring stigma, which has its own social costs. Examples of these diseases are AIDS, cancer, or stroke. The stigma appears because of the changes in physical activity, professional role, or self-concept (Lubkin and Larsen, 2006: 48). There are three types of stigma in the community:

1. *Physical deformity stigma.* This stigma is a deficit between the norms of a perfect physical condition and actual physical condition. Some diseases cause changes in appearance or physical function, such as disabilities. Even aging naturally raises stigma, for example, that an old person will find it difficult to hear. Older individuals can refuse to buy an electronic listening device to avoid the stigma of being perceived as elderly. Therefore, economically, there is no cost of electronic hearing aids, but there is a cost due to hearing problems in the elderly who refuse to wear a hearing aid.

2. *Character assassination.* A stigma like this appears in several diseases such as HIV/AIDS, alcoholism, mental illness, and sexually transmitted diseases. Many people believe that people with these diseases are guilty and

deserve punishment for their illness because they did not comply with social norms in the community. Again, the fear of experiencing stigma becomes one of the main barriers for individuals to get health services and, therefore, has an impact on the economic aspects of the disease.

3. *Prejudice.* Prejudice is the perception of a person's condition in terms of labels of race, religion, or nationality of people who are seen as having lower status because of their individual characteristics. Prejudices bring about discrimination.

A stigma has an effect on indirect and direct costs because it affects health behavior, as well as the sick role of the person. These impacts can be, among others (Lubkin and Larsen, 2006: 55):

1. *Skipping is pretending not to be sick.* Examples of the skipping effect are a person refusing to wear hearing aids or being unwilling to take an HIV or diabetes test. A person can also use this strategy by explaining that the symptoms he/she has are not because of a specific disease but are due to other causes, such as fighting or accidents. Economically, this will reduce the direct costs such as maintenance or medication costs.

2. *Covering is preventing others from knowing the individual is experiencing the disease.* An example is to wear veils or long clothing to cover skin disease or laughing and joking to cover the pain and sadness. Economically, this affects the rise of other costs that are not medical costs but meet needs, such as the cost of longer clothes or a veil.

3. *Neglect is not responding to prejudices.* Some examples are those who suffer from a disability but try to gain achievements so people will say, "Even though he/she suffers from X, he/she is able to do Y." Another way is to declare one's illness openly in public but emphasize

the struggle to heal or cope with the illness. Economic aspects of neglect behavior may be the emergence of costs together with normal costs, or even greater costs, in order to prove that the individual is able to do something productive despite being hindered by illness.

4. *Resistance and rejection.* Resistance and rejection directly lead to rejecting the statements of medical professionals who provide disease diagnosis. This often occurs in cases of mental illnesses that are more difficult to diagnose. The effects of resistance can reduce direct costs but do not affect the increased risk of a disease that becomes more severe. From the social side, resistance can have positive effects for preventing stigma and is therefore able to lower indirect costs associated with stigma.

5. *Isolation is alienating oneself from the public.* Isolation can be individual, for example, staying alone in a room, or collective, for example, forming a special group consisting of fellow sufferers of a disease. Isolation has a negative impact because it prevents public health services for the individual in isolation, causing greater suppression or stigma and greater collective isolation. Individuals with disabilities, for example, generally feel more comfortable when they are among able-bodied people compared to being among people with disabilities because they see themselves as normal.

6. *Information management is the managing of information about the disease in the community in many ways.* An example is renaming a disease. Lepers can choose to state that they have neurodermatitis mycobacterium disease, which is synonymous but has a lower social burden than leprosy. Similarly, families with family members who have HIV/AIDS can keep the information from people who are not medical professionals and ask people to keep matters relating to the disease from the community.

The Proportion of Direct and Indirect Costs

The proportion of direct and indirect costs may vary depending on the patient's suffering. In older patients, generally the direct costs are the largest cost component because these people are already not very productive economically. Meanwhile, for younger patients, the component of indirect costs can be greater, although it must be balanced with efforts to recover as quickly as possible in order to be productive again, which causes large direct costs. Other factors that can determine the proportion of the direct costs other than age are comorbidities and immunodepression, duration of hospitalization, use of medication, and severity of the disease.

Meanwhile, factors determining the proportion of indirect costs are productive age and becoming a productive worker. Patients who are unemployed usually see illness as having as more serious effect on them, feel that illness lasts for a longer time, and report more symptoms and emotional responses. Meanwhile, people with jobs have a strong belief that they are able to control disease and understand disease better (Lubkin and Larsen, 2006: 27).

References

Fang, X., D. S. Brown, C. S. Florence, and J. A. Mercy. 2012. The economic burden of child maltreatment in the United States and implications for prevention. *Child Abuse & Neglect* 36(2), 156–165.
Lubkin, I. M. and P. D. Larsen. 2006. *Chronic Illness: Impact and Interventions*. Sudbury, MA: Jones & Bartlett Learning.
Panatto, D., N. L. Bragazzi, E. Rizzitelli, P. Bonanni, S. Boccalini, G. Icardi, R. Gasparini, and D. Amicizia. 2015. Evaluation of the economic burden of herpes zoster (HZ) infection. *Human Vaccines & Immunotherapeutics* 11(1), 245–262.

Chapter 7

Economical Aspects of Hospital-Acquired Infections

Introduction

Hospital-acquired infections (HAIs) are health incidents inflicted by the hospital itself (nosocomial). There are three health incidents that can be inflicted during someone's stay in the hospital: medical error (medication errors and procedural errors, such as foreign objects left internally after surgery, air embolisms, blood discrepancies, pressure ulcers, falling down and trauma, and bad glycemic control manifestation), nosocomial, and hospitalization (physical and mental disorders due to extremely long hospitalization) (Weisz et al., 2011). Nosocomial infections, or HAIs, affect the hospital's economy the most because they have a higher frequency than medical errors and hospitalization. The occurrence of an HAI is regrettable because hospitals should be centers of healing, not the source of disease.

Some examples of HAIs are ulcer infection due to urinary catheter insertion (Townsend, 2013: 25) and blood vessel infection due to nonsterile syringes (Shannon et al., 2006) that cause complications such as pancreatitis, gastroplasti, congenital heart failure, and respiratory failure.

However, HAIs are hard to avoid because they may originate as a consequence of caring complexity. The more complex it is to care for a patient, the greater the chance an error will happen, which results in another health problem. Indeed, there is a certain level to which an HAI can be avoided. Another factor that may inflict HAIs is poor quality of care, such as nonsterile syringes, fake drugs, diagnosis errors, excessive number of patients (Kutzin, 1993: 96), and others.

Implementation of Work Standardization

If HAIs are indeed caused by unhealthy hospital environmental factors, hospitals should be able to avoid them. The aim of avoiding HAIs can be accomplished by the implementation of work standardization and obedience to legal guides, which indeed as only a slogan to obtain profit from new patients, but is really based on daily performance. For example, hospitals can hire special nurses to monitor infections or HAI occurrence potential, as applied in England in 1959 (Pheysey, 1993: 174). Another example is washing hands well and cleaning health instruments with alcohol (Larson et al., 2015: 4). Maintaining an environment designed to be centered on patients' care would reduce complications such as HAIs, medication errors, and depression (Iezzoni and O'Day, 2006: 228). Only, HAIs caused by caring complexity are hard to avoid.

HAIs as a result of caring complexity also increase caring complexity, creating a cycle that is potentially continuous and fatal. For hospitals, there is a dilemma. HAI individually may increase the diagnosis-related group (DRG) index and thus increase the hospital's profit from medical treatment. However, on the other hand, this is not justified ethically, and if the public notices there are many occurrences of HAIs in a hospital, they would leave the hospital. This would cause lower quality and increase HAIs for those who were still loyal to the hospital. HAI sources from complexity then become HAI sources from poor medical service quality, and eventually bring about the death of the hospital and the patients.

Costs spent due to HAIs would depend on two things: when the HAI occurs during patient care and what complication manifestations occur. HAIs are a serious problem because one study estimates the level of HAI occurrence at 10%, or 1 in 10 patients in the hospital, at least in the United States in 2009 (DeCenzo et al., 2010: 205).

Economic Analysis of Hospital-Acquired Infections

An economic analysis on HAIs needs to be conducted because it can bring an understanding of the effect of care improvement for both the patients and hospital. One question that can be raised is: Do HAIs increase profits for the hospital? If affirmative, this is regrettable because hospitals can try to increase HAIs. Nevertheless, as explained in a study by Shannon et al. (2006), HAIs always bring disadvantages for the hospital. A study on the case of an HAI in the form of central line–associated bloodstream (CLAB) infections proves that hospitals incur losses due to HAI occurrence, although there is additional revenue from the increase in treatment.

It is estimated that 43% of total care costs for patients with HAIs in a hospital are due to HAI care and its complexity. This means the hospital spends 75% more for patients with HAIs than those without. Another question is: What economic impact is incurred by a hospital if it applies a program to abolish or reduce HAIs, for example, through an industrial system redesigning activity.

A concept in line with an HAI economic impact evaluation is the net operating margin (NOM). Hospital net operating margin is the difference between payments and expenses for every illness case complicated by an HAI. In other words, net operating margin is none other than profit obtained by the hospital from care of a disease and its complications. The calculation of NOM should examine in detail the profit obtained by the hospital and what costs are incurred by the hospital.

Hospital Costs Spent

Costs spent by the hospital include:

1. Direct costs
   a. Fixed costs, for example, bed days in the intensive care unit (ICU) and the cost of daily ventilator care involve employment costs for nursing and other health officer costs, such as respiratory therapists, including procedural costs as well, such as dialysis, endoscopies, radiologic procedures, and surgical procedures.
   b. Variable costs, for example, antibiotic costs, radiology and lab study costs, diagnostic costs, and therapeutic costs.
2. Indirect costs involve the cost of loan services and overhead corporate costs. Indirect costs are generally not calculated in NOM calculations.

It is crucial to compare NOMs in cases with and without HAIs. Therefore, the study should compare hospital costs and revenue from patients with HAIs and patients without HAIs. A control group should be used in this procedure. Control is performed by establishing a study group with similarities in age, admission diagnosis, comprehensive clinical admission severity group (CC-ASG), and payer. The Student's t-test should be used to compare patients with factors of age, admission diagnosis, and disease severity.

This is to detect the most important cause of HAIs. If those factors are significant, this means there is a difference between patients who acquire HAIs and those who don't based on age, diagnosis, or disease severity; thus, these factors can be considered HAI risk factors. Otherwise, it can be concluded that HAIs are caused by errors in the process rather than disease complexity.

The Importance of Hospital-Acquired Infections

Why are HAIs important and deadly? There are three answers. First, hospitals are the most likely location for the occurrence of disease spread. Many patients with various conditions, especially infectious diseases, gather in a hospital. As noticed, infectious diseases can easily strike in a situation when many people with infectious diseases gather in one place with those who don't suffer from infectious diseases. As a result, without any means of quarantine, germs can spread quickly to those who don't suffer from related diseases. Moreover, if the disease exists in an environment out of the hospital, people generally realize what the infectious disease is and take preventive measures. In a hospital, because there are many kinds of infectious diseases, people cannot be certain what disease is spreading; thus, it is harder to take preventive measures.

Second, there are three types of humans who can be exposed to infectious diseases from patients: other patients, companions, and health workers. Out of those three, patients, especially those from vulnerable groups such as neonates, are the most vulnerable patients compared to health workers and companions. This vulnerability is due to low health conditions compared to companions who are in moderate health and medical workers who have "excellent" health.

Third, evolution causes bacteria in hospitals to become resistant to antibiotics. In environments outside hospitals, bacteria or other germs are exposed to various environmental pressures, so natural selection occurs and is not centralized, and evolution is slow.

In a hospital, natural selection pressure is specific. Common disease bacteria will be exposed continuously to natural selection pressure, especially in the form of antibiotic exposure. Say there are 1000 common bacteria exposed to antibiotics. From these 1000 bacteria, individual variations will cause the antibiotics to kill 900 and leave 100 stronger. Because 900 bacteria vanish, the remaining 100 strong bacteria have more space to develop. They breed easily and reach 1000 once more. These 1000 bacteria are no longer common bacteria; they are descendants of the 100 strong bacteria. The same antibiotics given to 1000 common bacteria are no longer effective for the 1000 strong bacteria. As a result, more effective antibiotics are given. This kills 900 bacteria but leaves 100 stronger bacteria. These 100 stronger bacteria are once again breed into 1000 bacteria, and so on. This means there is a battle between humans and bacteria, and the battlefield is hospitals. This will become severe until it produces bacteria that are totally resistant to all kinds of antibiotics. They are called antibiotic-resistant bacteria (ARB). The most common bacterium that mutates into ARB is *Staphylococcus aureus*. This super bacterium, when it infect patients, causes a higher caring cost compared to common patient care.

As an overview, one study estimates there were 2 million HAIs in the United States in 1995, one-quarter of which were due to antibiotic resistance of *S. aureus*. Since it was discovered in 1946, penicillin has been able to fight *S. aureus*. However, this *S. aureus* is resistant to penicillin and should be treated using methicillin, which has a higher cost. About half of *S. aureus* is then resistant to methicillin and thus should be treated with the higher-cost vancomycin. About 22% of *S. aureus* is resistant to vancomycin and should be treated with Zyvox (linezolid), which was just found in 1999 and has an even higher cost (Palumbi, 2001: 18).

A similar thing is found in *Enterococcus faecium* infections as well. This can no longer be denied. The cost of antibiotics eventually went from only Rp 18–24 thousand per ampule to about Rp 200 thousand per ampule (Republika, November 12, 2010). Today, the market cost for the cheapest penicillin, amoxicillin, is $9; methicillin is $109; vancomycin is $326; and Zyvox $3.620, which consists of 20 vials.

Incremental Cost-Effectiveness Ratio

The price of medicine is only one part of its economical aspects. To measure more comprehensively, the incremental cost-effectiveness ratio (ICER) can be used. ICER is calculated by comparing the difference of cost to effectiveness, with the formula:

$$\text{ICER} = \frac{\text{Cost}_{d1} - \text{Cost}_{d2}}{\text{Effectiveness}_{d1} - \text{Effectiveness}_{d2}}$$

This equation means a successful treatment using a medicine will be better than its comparator if the treatment with this medicine is more expensive but results in better effectiveness than the comparator medicine, or treatment cost with this medicine is cheaper and more effective. Meanwhile, if treatment costs with the medicine is more expensive but not effective, then the medicine is considered not feasible economically.

This is common because treatment costs with cheaper medicines and higher effectiveness should be the most economical because that means high-quality medicine is available for all people, or service costs with expensive medicine are expected to be more effective than cheap medicine because the additional value of the health aspect is considered apart from the effectiveness; otherwise, there would be no reason for people to buy expensive medicine. If the cost of medicine is higher, the treatment cost would be cheaper. Total cost tends to include cheap medicine and expensive treatment. Furthermore, even after being treated, if it turns out that patients have died with cheap medicine but were healed with more expensive medicine, then the greatest effectiveness should be based on expensive medicine that heals rather than cheap medicine that does not. If cheap medicine is more capable of healing than expensive medicine, the result of the calculation would be a negative value, which means cheap medicine is more effective.

For instance, Tan et al. (2014) calculated ICER for linezolid against vancomycin on a nosocomial pneumonic sufferer with an infection of penicillin-resistant *Staphylococcus aureus*. Although the cost of linezolid (Zyvox) is far higher than vancomycin, 453 yuan compared to 309 yuan, Zyvox also has an effectiveness of 54.8% compared to vancomycin, which has an effectiveness of only 44.9%. With this result, ICER is estimated for several cities in Tiongkok. In Beijing, the cost of inpatient medicine for vancomycin is 9608 yuan (Rp 18.92 million). The total cost of linezolid is 76,709 yuan (Rp 151.10 million). This means the cost of treatment for expensive medicine is less than the cost of treatment for cheap medicine. In line with this, effectiveness is measured by the proportion of patients who are successfully cured, which is 62.9% with linezolid but only 60.2% with vancomycin.

The result for ICER is 1899. This value is equal to the increased possibility of cured patients by 2.7%, with an additional cost of 51 yuan (Rp 100 thousand). This is positive, which means linezolid is more effective in cost than vancomycin.

References

DeCenzo, D. A., S. P. Robbins, and S. L. Verhulst. 2010. *Fundamentals of Human Resource Management.* Hoboken, NJ: John Wiley & Sons.

Iezzoni, L. I. and B. O'Day. 2006. *More Than Ramps: A Guide to Improving Health Care Quality and Access for People with Disabilities.* Oxford, UK: Oxford University Press.

Kutzin, B. H. 1993. *Public Hospitals in Developing Countries; Resource Use, Cost, and Financing.* Baltimore, MD: Johns Hopkins University Press.

Larson, T., R. Gudavalli, D. Prater, and S. Sutton. 2015. Critical analysis of common canister programs: A review of cross-functional considerations and health system economics. *Current Medical Research and Opinion* 31(4), 853–860.

Palumbi, S. R. 2001. Humans as the world's greatest evolutionary force. *Science* 293(5536), 1786–1790.

Pheysey, D. C. 1993. *Organizational Cultures: Types and Transformations.* New York: Taylor & Francis.

Shannon, R. P., B. Patel, D. Cummins, A. H. Shannon, G. Ganguli, and Y. Lu. 2006. Economics of central line-associated bloodstream infections. *American Journal of Medical Quality* 21(6 suppl), 7S–16S.

Tan, S. C., X. Wang, B. Wu, H. Kang, Q. Li, Y. Chen et al. 2014. Cost-effectiveness of linezolid versus vancomycin among patients with methicillin-resistant *Staphylococcus aureus* confirmed nosocomial pneumonia in China. *Value in Health Regional Issues* 3, 94–100.

Townsend, W. 2013. Innovation and the perception of risk in the public sector. *International Journal of Organizational Innovation* (Online), 5(3), 21.

Weisz, U., W. Haas, J. M. Pelikan, and H. Schmied. 2011. Sustainable hospitals: A socio-ecological approach. *GAIA-Ecological Perspectives for Science and Society* 20(3), 191–198.

Chapter 8

Hospital Resource Management

Introduction

Hospital resource management is an activity directed toward work that produces efficiency. Efficiency means that the resources put in produce the maximum output. One hundred percent efficiency means all resources are successfully converted into output. The process that bridges input into output is resources, so it is said to be impossible to reach 100% efficiency. Management's task is keeping efficiency high and as close as possible to 100%. This is performed by, for instance, maintaining no waste in the process. Waste would reduce efficiency and disadvantage the hospital.

An inefficient hospital is characterized by various wastes. Included in this waste is waste of work. For instance, a hospital may charge high fees for patients with stitches, whereas patients with similar conditions who are treated with similar resources spend far less at a community health center. This indicates that the hospital is not efficient.

There are three kinds of efficiency that can be used as indicators for hospital resource management: technical efficiency, economic efficiency, and scale efficiency.

Technical Efficiency

Technical efficiency is the input ratio against the output with mixed input. For instance, output in terms of inpatients has input in the form of various combinations of doctors' time, treatment, and diagnostic work. The question is how much of the doctor's time, treatment, and diagnostic work should be used to produce the shortest bed day.

A hospital can be inefficient technically if it uses certain resources but produces a lower output than it should. For instance, if there is a certain number of doctors, nurses, supplies, and rooms, it may turn out that the number of outpatients is less than expected. Likewise, a hospital is technically inefficient if it achieves a certain output target with more resources than it should be using, for instance, with medicine administration more than it should be for outpatients.

Hospital technical efficiency can be viewed as an indicator of hospital performance. Formally, it can be stated as a ratio between weighted output and weighted input. This is because both output and input can be varied. Technical efficiency occurs if (1) there is an output increase based on a series of inputs and (2) there is an input decrease to achieve a series of outputs when waste is abolished (Dalmau-Atattodona and Puig-Junoy, 1998: 458).

Hospital technical efficiency can be affected by internal and external factors. For external factors, market structure factors, ownership, and regulations may cause technical inefficiency. For internal factors, indeed, the process that occurs in using resources to produce output may cause inefficiency.

Mathematically, the calculation of technical efficiency can be expressed as follows (Dalmau-Atattodona and Puig-Juny, 1998: 458): A hospital uses several inputs, $x = (x_1 \ldots x_n) \in R^N+$, to produce output $y = (y_1 \ldots y_M) \in R^M+$. The technical efficiency can be obtained with the optimization function of TE (x,y) = min (which is efficiency; if it is 1, then efficiency is achieved, while if <1, inefficiency occurs. $L(y)$ is a family set of inputs, defined by $L(y) = \{x: (x,y) \in GR\}$, $y \in R^M+$, and GR is the GR graph = (x,y) meaning x can produce y). This means that of some inputs and some outputs, there is an efficient bridge set so the shortest path is from x to y (Dalmau-Atattodona and Puig-Junoy, 1998: 459).

Economic Efficiency

Economic efficiency is an aim to have the most economical input to achieve an output (Newbrander et al., 1992: 15). Because two inputs may have the same cost, a hospital can be economically efficient but not technically efficient. There would be some combinations of inputs where the cost is the same that can achieve desirable outputs.

Economic efficiency can be achieved if disutility phenomena are avoided. Disutility phenomena occur when a resource is not used as it is, so the cost spent to produce the resource is wasted and fails to produce output. In line with this, economic efficiency can be achieved by minimizing cost per patient as well. The output can be measured by cost, income, profit, or anything pursued by the production department.

This complicates things because, actually, the aim of a hospital is treatment quality, and it is difficult to measure financially.

Mathematically, economic efficiency is measured as the ratio of predicted minimum cost against actual cost. If a hospital performs several activities, then economic efficiency is aggregated by summing the economic efficiency of every production activity. The formula of economic efficiency (EE) is expressed as:

$$EE = \frac{\widehat{TC}}{TC} = \frac{\sum_{i=1}^{n} \hat{C}_i}{\sum_{i=1}^{n} C_i} = s_1 x E_1 + s_2 x E_2 + \cdots + s_n x E_n$$

where TC/TC is the ratio of predicted total cost to total actual cost, $E_i = C_i/C_i$ is economic efficiency in activity production of i, and $s_1 = C_i / \sum_{i=1}^{n} C_1$ is the total cost segment of activity I (Eckerman, 2004: 23).

In line with the formula above, aggregate economic efficiency would always be lower than individual economic efficiency. For instance, if there are two inpatient installations in hospital C, each has a cost segment of 50%; meanwhile, hospitalization A has an efficiency of 0.9, and hospitalization B has an efficiency of 0.6; then, aggregate economic efficiency is only $= 0.9 \times 0.5 + 0.6 \times 0.5 = 0.75$.

If compared to another hospital, say, hospital D, that makes hospitalization efficiency A only 0.8 and hospitalization efficiency B 0.5. However, the cost segment for hospitalization A is 90% and hospitalization segment B is 10%. This means the aggregate economic efficiency is greater: 0.77. This situation causes a paradox because a hospital with inefficient activity has greater economic efficiency in aggregate. In the literature, this paradox is called the Fox paradox.

The Fox paradox occurs due to considerations against the cost segment. The cost segment is the number of patients who come for treatment. This is an external factor because hospitals cannot determine how many patients come to it. However, the aggregate economic efficiency equation claims that two hospitals with the same economic efficiency on an installation would have different efficiencies on the aggregate level due to the impact of the cost segment difference. Private hospitals can control this external factor more if they can send patients to installations they possess and, although it is slightly unethical, refuse patients if they potentially reduce aggregate efficiency.

Scale Efficiency

Scale efficiency relates to the whole system in producing output using the lowest cost. Scale efficiency can be achieved in the short and long term. In the long term, all inputs can be varied, while in the short term, certain inputs, such as bed and facility capacities, are fixed, so variation is more limited.

Scale diseconomy occurs if the scale of a hospital is larger or smaller than its optimum scale. For instance, if scale calculation considers the optimum number of beds 120 units, then a hospital with either 200 or 80 beds is considered inefficient in scale. This is viewed from the return scale that we discussed in the previous chapter. In the case of 200 beds, the optimum point has been passed, while in the case of 80 beds, the optimum point has not been passed.

Scale efficiency in the health service industry is strongly affected by market and institutional obstacles. Competition among hospitals as well as hospital institutions can hamper hospitals in working at the optimum scale (Masiye, 2007: 4).

Scale efficiency is basically the ratio of the technical efficiency value against the constant return to scale (CRS) assumption to the technical efficiency value in the variable return to scale (VRS) assumption. Mathematically, this scale efficiency equation is:

$$SE_j = \frac{TE_j(y_j, x_j, CRS)}{TE_j(y_j, x_j, VRS)}$$

The equation above means that SE scale efficiency in hospital j is the technical efficiency (TE) ratio of hospital j, with input x and output y on the CRS assumption against the technical efficiency of hospital j and input x and output y on the VRS assumption.

Just remember that general equation of technical efficiency is:

$$TE(x, y) = \min\{\theta : \theta x \in L(y)\}$$

To minimize θ, CRS has two obstacles (Masiye, 2007: 4):

$$\sum_{j=1}^{J} z_j y_{mj} \geq y_j$$

$$\sum_{j=1}^{J} z_j x_{mj} \geq \theta x_{nj}$$

where z is the intensity variable used in the DEA model to determine efficient production, j is the serial number of the hospital, x_{nj} is the output n used by hospital j, y_{mj} is the output m produced by hospital j, m is the output, and n is the input. In other words, a hospital has m output, which is $y_j = y_{1j}$, $y_{2j}, \ldots, y_{mj}$, and n input ($x_j = x_{1j}, x_{2j}, \ldots, x_{nj}$).

The above equation means that the sum of the multiplication of constant z by the sum of the output produced by the hospital should be greater than or equal to the total output, and the sum of the multiplication of constant z by the sum of the input produced by the hospital should be greater than or equal to the technical efficiency multiplied by the total input. The VRS assumption adds one more obstacle, the convexity obstacle, in which the z value should be equal to 1 (Masiye, 2007: 4):

$$\sum_{j=1}^{J} z = 1$$

The VRS assumption should be used if the hospital scale is possibly affected by institutional or geographical obstacles, while the CRS assumption can be used if the hospital scale is possibly affected by market obstacles. The VRS assumption guarantees that every hospital is compared with another hospital with a similar scale (Masiye, 2007: 1).

The technical efficiency value with the VRS assumption would be greater than the technical efficiency with the CRS assumption. Only if the technical efficiency value with the VRS assumption is as much as the technical efficiency value with the CRS assumption has the hospital achieved scale efficiency. If the VRS is larger, then efficiency has not been achieved.

The Relation among Efficiencies

A hospital manager may face more than one inefficiency problem. The aim to increase one efficiency sometimes leads to sacrificing another efficiency. For example, hospital A conducts lab tests manually, although it has an autoanalyzer device, and hospital B conducts lab tests with an autoanalyzer while doctors prepare and conduct the test, then report it. Hospital A is technically inefficient because the inputs (staff and devices) are not combined correctly to produce output (test results), but it is efficient economically because the cost to conduct the lab test is so low because it does not use an autoanalyzer device. If the hospital decides to add staff to conduct lab tests, then the technical inefficiency is far bigger, not smaller.

Hospital B is technically efficient because it is using the facilities correctly but economically inefficient because doctors conduct the test; it should be conducted by lab technicians. Furthermore, both hospitals are inefficient in scale because neither is working with the correct combination with the lowest cost.

The following graphic (Figure 8.1) further explains the relationship of technical, economic, and scale efficiencies. This graphic assumes that the output is in the form of patient days,

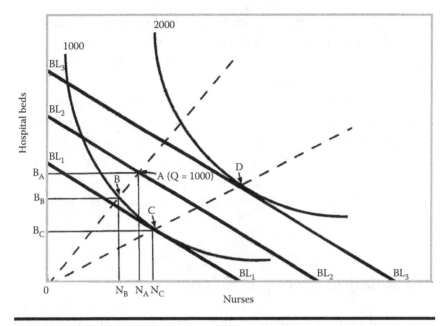

Figure 8.1 Technical, economy, and scale efficiencies. (Adapted from Newbrander, W., H. Barnum, and J. Kutzin. 1992. *Hospital Economics and Financing in Developing Countries*. Geneva: World Health Organization.)

and the input is in the form of beds and nurses. There are two curves (isoquants) in the figure: the curves of 1000 patient days and 2000 patient days. Each point in the curve indicates a technically efficient point.

Point A is not technically efficient because it uses more beds and nurses to achieve 1000 patient days. If A is moved to B, located on the 1000 isoquant curve, then there is a technical efficiency increase.

The straight line is the isocost line, which is the line indicating the combination of the number of beds and nurses that can be purchased with a similar cost. There are three budgets, BL_1, BL_2, and BL_3; getting farther from the center point indicates the higher total budget. Point B is technically efficient because it is located on the 1000 isoquant, but it is not economically efficient because it is located on a straight line. The

1000 isoquant actually intersects with three lines, but the best point is the point with the smallest budget, which is point C on the BL_1 line. Thus, the shift from point B to point C indicates an economic efficiency increase.

Furthermore, the hospital could consider creating 2000 patient days. To make it technically efficient, point C should move to a point on the 2000 isoquant. This point should also be an economically efficient point, which means it intersects the straight line. There is only one straight line passing the 2000 isoquant, BL_3, and the point of tangency is point D. Thus, movement from point C to point D would indicate greater scale efficiency.

References

Dalmau-Atarrodona, E. and J. Puig-Junoy. 1998. Market structure and hospital efficiency: Evaluating potential effects of deregulation in a National Health Service. *Review of Industrial Organization* 13(4), 447–466.

Eckermann, S. 2004. Hospital performance including quality: Creating economic incentives consistent with evidence-based medicine. PhD dissertation. University of New South Wales.

Masiye, F. 2007. Investigating health system performance: An application of data envelopment analysis to Zambian hospitals. *BMC Health Services Research* 7, 58.

Newbrander, W., H. Barnum, and J. Kutzin. 1992. *Hospital Economics and Financing in Developing Countries*, Geneva: World Health Organization.

Chapter 9

Economy Scale of Hospitals

Introduction

There is a dilemma in the development of a hospital, namely whether it is better to build one large hospital or build two small hospitals. At first, building a large hospital looks better than building two small hospitals, as this will be more efficient. Hospitals require huge capital investment in buildings, tools, and staff. One large building can be more efficient than two small buildings because some parts of the building can be used together, as well as the tools and staff. However, a small hospital also has its own advantages. A large hospital has a high complexity and is, therefore, more difficult to run smoothly than smaller hospitals.

Of course, it is better to build small hospitals to run than a chaotic and messy large hospital. Studies have generally found that the ideal size of a hospital is 100–200 beds (Ferguson et al., 1996). More or less than this will have problems of diseconomy of scale, but a more thorough study needs to be done because it will depend on the context of where the hospital is located.

In addition to the scale dilemma above, there is also a scope dilemma, such as whether the treatment of inpatients and outpatients should be combined. On the one hand, it seems better to combine both facilities because physicians can move more efficiently in serving inpatients and outpatients. Inpatients can also be given final service as outpatients for the next visit. Similarly, outpatients can be immediately transferred to inpatients when it is absolutely necessary. On the other hand, the mixing of patients can be confusing, and outpatient operation may be hampered by inpatient activities and vice versa.

The two dilemmas above are a problem of resource allocation, which has been discussed before. In line with this, this problem can be solved by the preparation of a cost function that looks at the relationship between the cost and output of the hospital. The cost function discussed in this chapter is more complex than that exemplified previously because it involves more variables.

This function is called the plural product model. In the plural product model, the total cost is the input cost function and the output level of a number of products, such as care days and outpatient visits. The plural product model has coefficient estimates for each product and involves the interaction rate of each product to measure the economy of scope.

Economy of Scale

The relationship between the cost and scale can be in the short or long term. A short-term function acts in order for the number of beds not to change, and all the efficiency advantages are collected on the variable factors. This advantage is called short-run returns to the variable factor (SRVF). The SRVF is formulated as follows (Barnum and Kutzin, 1993):

$$\text{SRVF} = \frac{C}{\left[\sum_{i=1}^{m} \text{MC}_i\, Y_i\right]}$$

where C is the total variable cost function, defined by:

$$C = e^{a_0 + a_1 \text{beds}} e^{f(Y,X)}$$

Y is a vector of hospital products, such as admissions, outpatient visits, and diagnostic examinations; X is a vector of independent variables that shifts the cost function, such as the area where the hospital is located and the hospital category.

MC is the marginal cost of admission or outpatient visits (or any product with a variable of linear, quadratic, cubic, and interactions), formulated by:

$$\text{MC}_i = C(b_{1i} + 2b_{2i}\, Y_i + 3\, b_{3i}\, Y_i^2 + b_{1*2}\, Y_j)$$

where j is the outpatient visits if i is the admission and vice versa. For the other output marginal cost besides outpatient and admission, MC follows the formula:

$$\text{MC}_k = Cb_k$$

The b coefficient itself is the coefficients estimated from the equations that become estimates of the cost function, which is formulated into a natural log function, namely:

$$\ln C = a_0 + a_1 \text{beds} + b_{11} Y_1 + b_{21} Y_1^2 + b_{31} Y_1^3 + b_{12} Y_2$$

$$+ b_{22} Y_2^2 + b_{32} Y_2^3 + b_{1*2} Y_1 Y_2 + \sum_{k=3}^{n} b_k Y_k + \sum_{l=1}^{m} c_l X_l$$

where Y_1 is the number of admissions and Y_2 is the number of outpatient visits.

In accordance with the definitions above, the SRVF equation can be changed to:

$$SRVF = \cfrac{1}{\left[\sum_{i=1}^{2} Y_i(b_{1i} + 2\,b_{2i}\,Y_i + 3\,b_{3i}\,Y_i^2 + b_{1*2}\,Y_j) + \sum_{k=3}^{m} Y_k b_k\right]}$$

If the SRVF value is greater than 1, then the output level is less than the most efficient level, while if it is less than 1, then the output level is greater than the most efficient level.

Furthermore, for the long-term function, the number of beds will also change along with other factors so that efficiency can increase. This long-term function is called economy of scale (EOS), defined as (Barnum and Kutzin, 1993):

$$EOS = \cfrac{(1 - \sigma_{C,beds})}{\left[\sum_{i=1}^{m} \sigma_{C,Y_i}\right]}$$

where $\sigma_{a,b}$ is the elasticity of a to b. σ_{c,y_i} is the multiplication result of the Y_i and Y_i/C ratio, so the EOS equation can be rewritten to:

$$EOS = \cfrac{(1 - a_1\ beds)}{\left[\sum_{i=1}^{2} Y_i(b_{1i} + 2\,b_{2i}\,Y_i + 3\,b_{3i}\,Y_i^2 + b_{1*2}\,Y_j) + \sum_{k=3}^{m} Y_k b_k\right]}$$

As in the SRVF interpretation, if the value of EOS is greater than 1, then the output level is less than the most efficient level, while if it is less than 1, then the output level is greater than the most efficient level.

Economy of Scope

Economy of scope measures the relationship between costs and product mix. The product mix, for example, is inpatient and outpatient care and whether it is cheaper to combine both or cheaper if they are separated. The equation for the economy of scope (Scope) is (Barnum and Kutzin, 1993):

$$\text{Scope}_s = \frac{\left[C(Y_s) + C(Y_{n-s}) + C(Y)\right]}{C(Y)}$$

which can be converted into the following equation:

$$\text{Scope}_2 = \frac{-2b_{1*2}Y_1Y_2}{\sum_{i=1}^{2} Y_i(b_{1i} + 2b_{2i}Y_i + 3b_{3i}Y_i^2 + b_{1*2}Y_j)}$$

In the above equation, the coefficient b_{1*2} determines the sign; if negative, it means that there is economy of scope, while if the coefficient is positive, it means that there is diseconomy of scope. Therefore, if this value is greater than 0, then it is more efficient to combine inpatient and outpatient care, while if it is less than 0, then it is more efficient to separate inpatient and outpatient care.

Application

There are several studies on the hospital cost function at the state level. Carey (1997) examined the scope of the United States. A study by Weaver and Deolalikar (2004) calculates the economy of scale and scope of hospitals in a developing country, namely Vietnam. In this study, the dependent variable that becomes the total costs variable is the total expenditures of the staff (salaries, allowances, and bonuses); drugs and medical supplies; maintenance and repairs; and other expenses such as sanitation, utilities, fuel, medical records, secondary education (human capital investment), and business travel. The purchase of equipment is not counted. Bed is the size of capital stock estimated as a single variable and variables with an interaction rate. Inpatient care is measured by admissions and inpatient days. The researchers also weighed different case mixes in each hospital, measured by the index of case complexity by the formula:

$$\text{index}_i = \text{ALOS}_i \left(\frac{\text{OCC}_i}{\text{OCC}_s} \right)$$

where ALOS_i is the average length of stay in hospital i, OCC_i is hospital i's occupancy rate, and OCC_s is the average hospital occupancy rate that becomes the sample of the study.

Other output variables besides inpatient care are outpatient visits, surgery, lab tests, and X-rays. The vector of independent variables that shifts the cost function includes variables for each hospital category, with the exception of provincial public hospitals, and for each area of the country, with the exception of the northern mountains.

The researchers then calculated the equation Ln C above and tested the multicollinearity and heteroscedasticity using the Cook and Weisberg test (Breusch-Pagan test) that checks whether the residual of the cost function correlates with the independent variable (Judge et al., 1980). Heteroscedasticity is necessary to check to find the possible effect on the calculation of variable significance. The standard error is calculated by the Huber–White method.

The researchers then calculated the marginal cost (MC_i), predicted by the smearing factor for the normal distribution of the residual heteroscedastic. The prediction was tested with the kurtosis and skewness statistics to determine whether the distribution was normal. The smearing factor is the prediction value of the squared residual regressed on the independent variables in the cost function. Marginal cost prediction is formulated by:

$$E(C) = e^{a_0 + a_1 \text{beds}} \, e^{f(Y,X)} e^{\text{smear}/2}$$

Based on the variables above, the equation is:

$$\text{In } C = a_0 + a_1\text{beds} + b_{11}Y_1 + b_{21}Y_1^2 + b_{31}Y_1^3 + b_{12}Y_2$$

$$+ b_{22}Y_2^2 + b_{32}Y_2^3 + b_{1*2}Y_1Y_2 + \sum_{k=3}^{n} b_k Y_k + \sum_{l=1}^{m} c_l X_l$$

where $n = 6$ and $m = 11$, and it can be transformed into:

$$\text{In } C = a_0 + a_1\text{beds} + b_{11}Y_1 + b_{21}Y_1^2 + b_{31}Y_1^3 + b_{12}Y_2 + b_{22}Y_2^2 + b_{32}Y_2^3$$
$$+ b_{1*2}Y_1Y_2 + b_3Y_3 + b_4Y_4 + b_5Y_5 + b_6Y_6 + c_1X_1 + c_2X_2 + c_3X_3$$
$$+ c_4X_4 + c_5X_5 + c_6X_6 + c_7X_7 + c_8X_8 + c_9X_9 + c_{10}X_{10} + c_{11}X_{11}$$

where:
Y_1 = Number of admissions
Y_2 = Number of outpatient visits
Y_3 = Operations
Y_4 = X-rays
Y_5 = Test labs
Y_6 = Complexity index case

where:
$X_1, X_2, X_3, X_4, X_5, X_6$ = Types of hospitals, namely general hospital (GH) centers, specialized hospital (SH) centers, SH provincial hospitals, district hospitals, subdistrict hospitals, and other hospitals.
$X_7, X_8, X_9, X_{10}, X_{11}$ = Geographic regions, namely Red River Delta, North Coast, Central Coast, Central Highlands, Southeast, and Mekong River Delta.

EOS is estimated by the equation:

$$\text{EOS} = \frac{(1 - a_1\text{beds})}{\left[\sum_{i=1}^{2} Y_i(b_{1i} + 2b_{2i}Y_i + 3b_{3i}Y_i^2 + b_{1*2}Y_j) + \sum_{k=3}^{m} Y_k b_k \right]}$$

into:

$$EOS = \frac{(1 - a_1 beds)}{\left[\begin{array}{l} Y_1(b_{11} + 2b_{21}Y_1 + 3b_{31}Y_1^2 + b_{1*2}Y_2) + Y_2(b_{12} + 2b_{22}Y_2 \\ + 3b_{32}Y_2^2 + b_{1*2}Y_1) + b_3Y_3 + b_4Y_4 + b_5Y_5 + b_6Y_6 \end{array}\right]}$$

estimated for each type of hospital.

In cases where the economy of scale is negative, it can be caused by the misspecification of the variable costs function due to the amount of certain hospital types being too low. Corrections can be done by respecifying by adding elements interactions for the bed and hospital categories. As a result, the numerator on the EOS equation changes from $(1 - a_1 beds)$ to:

$$(1 - a_1 beds - a_2 X_1 beds - a_3 X_2 beds - a_4 X_3 beds - a_5 X_4 beds \\ - a_6 X_5 beds)$$

Coefficients a_2, a_3, a_4, a_5, and a_6 are recalculated through a new cost function, so that the equation becomes:

$$\begin{aligned} \ln C = {} & a_0 + a_1 beds + a_2 X_1 beds + a_3 X_2 beds + a_4 X_3 beds + a_5 X_4 beds \\ & + a_6 X_5 beds + b_{11}Y_1 + b_{21}Y_1^2 + b_{31}Y_1^3 + b_{12}Y_2 + b_{22}Y_2^2 + b_{32}Y_2^3 \\ & + b_{1*2}Y_1Y_2 + b_3Y_3 + b_4Y_4 + b_5Y_5 + b_6Y_6 + c_1X_1 + c_2X_2 + c_3X_3 \\ & + c_4X_4 + c_5X_5 + c_6X_6 + c_7X_7 + c_8X_8 + c_9X_9 + c_{10}X_{10} + c_{11}X_{11} \end{aligned}$$

The interaction coefficient may indicate a negative sign. This will indicate that the type of the hospital is operating close to the long-term equity, especially if it is close to 0. The value of economy of scale can be recalculated and the results will be positive. The original cost equation with interaction is tested by the likelihood ratio test. If it is significant, it means that the new interaction equation is better than the original cost equation that uses only one bed variable.

Economy of scope is also estimated for each type of hospital by the following equation:

$$\text{Scope}_2 = \frac{-2b_{1*2}Y_1Y_2}{\begin{array}{l} Y_1(b_{11} + 2b_{21}Y_1 + 3b_{31}Y_1^2 + b_{1*2}Y_2) \\ + Y_2(b_{12} + 2b_{22}Y_2 + 3b_{32}Y_2^2 + b_{1*2}Y_1) \end{array}}$$

References

Barnum, H. and J. Kutzin. 1993. *Public Hospitals in Developing Countries: Resource Use, Cost, and Financing.* Baltimore, MD: Johns Hopkins University Press.

Carey, K. 1997. A panel data design for estimation of hospital cost functions. *Review of Economics and Statistics* 79(3), 443–453.

Ferguson, B., N. Rice, D. Sykes, V. Aletras, A. Eastwood, T. Sheldon et al. 1996. Hospital volume and health care outcomes, costs and patient access. *Effective Health Care* 2(8), 1–16.

Judge, G. G., W. E. Griffiths, R. C. Hill, and T.-C. Lee. 1980. *Theory and Practice of Econometrics.* New York: Wiley.

Weaver, M. and A. Deolalikar. 2004. Economies of scale and scope in Vietnamese hospitals. *Social Science & Medicine* 59(1), 199–208.

Chapter 10

Hospital Human Resources Development

Introduction

Hospital human resources (HR) development is crucial because it provides an excellent HR supply, which is more economical than hiring professional workers directly from another hospital who have retired or job seekers with high-quality specifications and certifications who are ready to work. For instance, in the United States, the cost to study medicine per year for undergraduate students was $40,000–$50,000 (Rp 524–655 million) in 1997. In 2012, it cost $278,300 (Rp 3.65 billion). Compared to Indonesia, this cost is far higher. At the University of Indonesia, the total cost for four years is only Rp 107 million, while for a private university, the average cost is Rp 150 million, which is 24 times cheaper than in the United States. In England, tuition fees reached ₤200,000 (Rp 3.45 billion) per student every year in 1997 and ₤298,000 (Rp 5.16 billion) per year in 2012 (Fitzgerald, 2012).

Training, as the main form of HR development, is indeed costly. Thus, it can be studied from a hospital's economic perspective.

The direct-cost components of training include (Fitzgerald, 2012):

1. Salary and advantages for training participants. The amount for this does not consider lost income because doctors should undergo training and cannot do practical work during it. This cost is considered an indirect cost in the aspect of unit productivity change.
2. Trainer costs and anything relevant to them. Relevant costs include, for example, training and procedural costs using instruments from training labs.
3. Training facilities, for example, a training lab. This cost comes from the use of a training lab, including all components in it.
4. Faculty development to develop a curriculum.
5. Administration of training participants and training programs.

Components of indirect costs include:

1. The difference in procedural time
2. The change in unit productivity
3. Variations in efficiency
4. The difference in the use of resources
5. Overhead costs related to faculty

The amount of this cost is then compared to the income obtained from specialist training practice in the hospital together with the training that occurs. A study by Fitzgerald et al. (2012) found that surgeons' income is 74.8% of (post training) surgeons' income. This income is too small, and they should be compensated based on their income if they have not received any training. The training cost itself was $47.97

in 2012. This cost is equal to the undergraduate tuition fee in 1997 and was only one-sixth of that by 2012.

For training to run optimally, there are three things to consider (Mochifefe, 2006: 74):

1. *Training participants.* Factors related to training participants that should be optimized are willingness, learning level, working experience, and work routines. Doctors or other staff members should be willing to take the training seriously. They should have a high learning capacity as well, that is, analytic capability, and so on. Working experience is required if the training is very specific. Otherwise, training should be started from a basic level, and it uses costs. Employee working routines should be considered because excessive work schedules may negatively affect the hospital income.
2. *Training.* Training factors that should be considered include preparation, teaching strategy, evaluation methods, trainer competence, and training content.
3. *Workplace.* The workplace is crucial to facilitate training transfer, which is the implementation of training results at the workplace. Factors of the workplace are culture, mentoring, directing, feedback, and opportunities for implementation. Employees who have been training with high costs would cause a deficit if they did not have the opportunity to implement the results of their training. That is why training is frequently required to prepare for work in the near future or to improve the current practice.

HR development is not only training. There should be at least 12 kinds of activity for HR development that can be offered by the hospital to the employees. Hospital HR development activities include:

1. Outside training: An employee may be sent twice for training outside of the hospital.

2. Study visits: This may be general or specific. Specific study visits include specialist personnel visits to other places with a specific purpose.
3. Academic conferences.
4. Internal training.
5. Meeting or training in certain divisions or units. This activity may be in the form of supervising or technical discussions on something new.
6. Specific group activity, which is a special interest club such as an English club, fitness club, alternative treatment club, as well as special training programs to develop emotional quotients.
7. Health education and study materials for patients and common people, such as a reading corner in every service unit.
8. Study support.
9. Activities with the government or the main company group.
10. Community development such as corporate social responsibility (CSR).
11. Primary health promotion involving volunteers and community leaders.
12. Customer service.

If the hospital then selects HR development by education, the hospital is confronted with different components of cost. Education takes longer than training but allows an employee to obtain more knowledge and skills than someone who takes only training. However, to obtain education for qualified health workers, employees are not only required to temporarily delay service activity at the hospital, they should also come to the area, or even another country, where the education is offered.

Costs included in education as private costs include:

1. *Primary costs.* These costs include:
    a. Registration costs and entry fees
    b. Semester costs
    c. Final task/lab/project/library costs

     d. Special costs
     e. University matriculation costs
     f. Test costs
  2. *Secondary costs.* These costs include:
     a. Internal costs consisting of books and materials, courses, study tours, lodging, and donations
     b. Additional costs consisting of the cost of tours, food, clothing, memberships, entertainment, and so on
  3. *Opportunity costs*

Hospitals may choose to construct an institution or division specified for training and education that internally develops hospital HR. Some hospitals are basically educational hospitals that have a double function. The working method of an educational hospital is different because it has its headquarters at a university, which is different from a hospital that constructs its own training and education institution, meaning the hospital is its own headquarters. In both cases, there are four kinds of costs that should be calculated.

These costs are called social costs, including (Devasia and Bai, 2005: 99):

  1. *Continuous/unplanned costs.* These costs include:
     a. Remuneration of lectures, nonlectures, and administration and education staff
     b. Test costs
     c. Other costs
  2. *Capital/planned costs.* These costs include:
     a. Land
     b. Buildings
     c. Instruments
     d. Libraries
     e. Laboratories
     f. Recreational land
     g. Auditoriums
     h. Maintenance costs

3. *Student aid costs.* These costs include:
    a. Semester cost concessions
    b. Scholarships
    c. Salaries during study
    d. Donations
    e. Indulgency costs
4. *Opportunity costs*

Based on the two kinds of costs, in internal HR develop-ment, hospitals should more or less endure both. Thus, the total cost for education as a form of hospital HR development is formulated by (Devasia and Bai, 2005: 105):

$$TC_E = \alpha_{Td} + \beta_{Ts}$$

where TC_E is the total cost for education, α_{Td} is the private cost, and β_{Ts} is the social cost.

On the other hand, for HR units and hospitals, there is an advantage from investment spent. The private advantages include (Devasia and Bai, 2005: 110):

1. *Direct advantages*
    a. Subsidies
    b. Future income expectations
2. *Secondary/indirect advantages*
    a. Savings
    b. Consumption expenditures
    c. Living quality
    d. Efficiency and proficiency
    e. Productivity
    f. Life expectancy
    g. Family size
    h. Social status
3. *Opportunistic advantages* include various advantages obtained by HR compared to other employees who do not have the same education

The social advantages obtained by the hospital and the common people include:

1. *Direct advantages*
   a. Primary direct advantages—Sources from anything paid by students/HR to get an education
   b. Secondary advantages—Sources from tax and employment income
2. *Indirect advantages*
   a. Net income from HR exports
   b. Savings/investments
   c. Consumption expenditures
3. *External advantages*
   a. Productivity
   b. Speed and efficiency
   c. Public qualities
   d. Social welfare
   e. Community size
   f. Poverty reduction
   g. Inequality reduction
   h. Unemployment reduction
   i. International outlook
   j. Cultural exchange, etc.
4. *Opportunistic advantages*
   a. Advantages of HR with varying education
   b. Not hiring important HR
   c. HR profligacy reduction
   d. Administration loss reduction, etc.

References

Devasia, M. D. and M. M. Bai. 2005. Economics of human resource planning with special reference to higher education in Kerala. Doctoral dissertation, Department of Economics, Coching University of Science and Technology, Kochi, Kerala, India.

Fitzgerald, J. E. F., P. Ravindra, M. Lepore, A. Armstrong, A. Bhangu, and C. A. Maxwell-Armstrong. 2013. Financial impact of surgical training on hospital economics: An income analysis of 1184 out-patient clinic consultations. *International Journal of Surgery* 11(5), 378–382.

Mochifefe, M. A. 2006. Human resource development in radiography education: A search for excellence in a time of change. Doctoral dissertation, University of Pretoria, South Africa.

Chapter 11

Methods of Improving the Quality of the Hospital

Introduction

There are many factors to take into consideration as well as factors that affect the quality of a hospital, as discussed earlier. It is time to talk about how to improve the quality of the hospital itself. In the literature of quality management, there are three common methods that are often used: Total Quality Management (TQM), Six Sigma, and Lean. All three methods can be used in the context of the hospital, and the third method also has economic aspects to be taken into account.

Total Quality Management, Six Sigma, and Lean

TQM, Six Sigma, and Lean are three concepts that overlap. They can be likened to the three blind men who see an elephant. The elephant is ideal quality management. The three blind men hold the tail, a leg, and an ear and say that quality management is like a snake (tail), a pole (leg), and a fan (ear). All three are right but only partially. A more complete picture, of course, is to say that it is an elephant. But because of human cognitive limitations, we can approach it only from a narrow perspective. Similarly, TQM, Six Sigma, and Lean can be seen as three things that become the elements of greater quality management, but because we do not know what ideal quality management is, we can formulate only partial quality management methods that only approach the elements of ideal quality management. It is no surprise that many parts of the three methods have similar aspects.

The definitions of each method are as follows (Andersson et al., 2006):

1. *TQM.* A management system that continues to evolve, consisting of values, methodologies, and tools with the aim to improve internal and external customer satisfaction with minimal resources.
2. *Six Sigma.* A business process that allows companies to improve their bottom line drastically and oversee daily business activities by minimizing waste and resources while increasing customer satisfaction.
3. *Lean.* A systematic approach to identifying and eliminating waste through continuous improvement, product distribution, and customer attraction in the pursuit of perfection.

From the definitions above, we know that the purpose of each of the three methods are more or less the same, which is to increase customer satisfaction and financial outcomes while reducing waste and resources. The third method also has the same history namely Japan, from the aftermath of World War II. We might think that all these methods were used by Japan to recover its economy after the destruction and defeat in the world war.

If we look more closely, the three methods are different in their hierarchies. TQM is the most common because it is a management system. It applies to any organization because management really works in any organization. Six Sigma is more specific because it is a business process, and Lean is the most specific because it is only a systematic approach. They can be linked to one another, with Lean at the center, as a systematic approach in a business process in a management system of an organization.

Since TQM is the most common, the objective of TQM is organizational performance in relation to the end goal of the holistic aspect, which is customer satisfaction. How is this achieved? By values, methodologies, and tools that work with minimal resources. Six Sigma is also lodged within TQM and works in the same way but with more specific objectives. Six Sigma posits that customer satisfaction is achieved with the increase of minimum standards to drastically minimize waste. The method emphasizes the process and supervision, which is a group of tools and methodologies. It no longer holds to certain values, such as TQM. Lean, as the most specific, views the main objective as the pursuit of perfection, and as a form of the pursuit of perfection, waste will no longer be minimized but should be eliminated. This is achieved through a continuous improvement process and product distribution to customers. Therefore, if we start from Lean thinking, it means Lean tries to pursue perfection, which in turn will increase the minimum standards drastically in order to achieve customer satisfaction. Lean eliminates waste, Six Sigma minimizes waste and resources, and TQM minimizes resources. Lean achieves its objectives by continuous improvement and product distribution to the customer, followed by supervision and Six Sigma processes, until both are enhanced by the values, methodologies, and tools from TQM.

To truly understand the three methods, the following is a visual representation of the three methods in one frame.

As shown in Figure 11.1, Six Sigma is nothing but a special form of TQM, since Six Sigma is entirely lodged within TQM with the starting point of input at the minimum resources and the output point in customer satisfaction. In addition to being seen as a specific form of TQM, Lean can also become the complement to Six Sigma. Note that Lean uses specific elements of the process and supervision, that is, continuous improvement and customer retention, not only to minimize waste, but to elim-inate waste entirely. As waste minimization has been enough to deliver a drastic increase of minimum standards, waste elimina-tion will also bring in more drastic changes and finally result in the same end, namely customer satisfaction, as well.

Let us highlight three things that become the core compo-nents of TQM: values, methodologies, and tools. Typical values held by TQM are orientation on the customer, process orien-tation, participation of all people, leadership commitment, con-tinuous improvement, and management by facts.

The methodology is a way of working within an organiza-tion in order to achieve those values. Meanwhile, the tool is

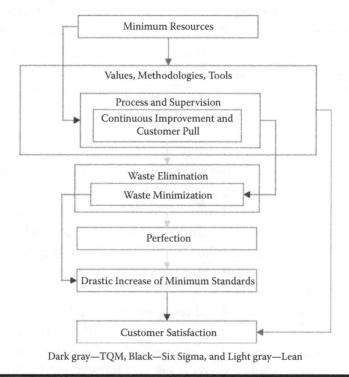

Dark gray—TQM, Black—Six Sigma, and Light gray—Lean

Figure 11.1 Total Quality Management, Six Sigma, and Lean.

a concrete and clear method and sometimes has a statistical basis to support decision making or data analysis. Universal values, methodologies, and tools in TQM can also be used by Six Sigma and Lean as long as they are relevant to the purpose of each method. In general, the methodology commonly used is the improvement cycle methodology. It is abbreviated as PDCA, namely:

1. *Plan*. Quality improvement plan
2. *Do*. Do or work on something that has been planned on a small scale
3. *Check*. Check whether the planned actions have achieved the goal
4. *Act*. Adopt the change, abandon it, or restart the cycle

Plan, Do, Check, Act

In 1993, after PDCA was formulated in 1950, it was refined into PDSA. PDSA replaces *Check* with *Study*. The reason is simply a matter of semantics, that is, the meaning of Check is more like "hold to check the errors," while Study means "learn to build knowledge." The use of Check is a translation of a Japanese term that is considered less accurate (Moen and Norman, 2009: 7).

In 1996, PDCA was redeveloped into a Model for Improvement. The development is done by adding three questions before doing the Plan. The three questions are:

1. What do we want to try to accomplish?
2. How do we know a change is an improvement?
3. What changes can we make that will produce progress?

After these three questions are answered, PDSA can be implemented.

The Seven Quality Control Tools

Meanwhile, the tools commonly used in TQM, Six Sigma, and Lean, are two groups called seven quality control tools and seven management tools. The seven quality control tools are: check sheet, histogram, Pareto chart, Ishikawa diagram, charts, scatter diagram, and control chart. Meanwhile, the seven management tools are affinity diagram, interrelationship diagram, systematic diagram, matrix diagram, matrix data analysis, process decision program chart, and arrow diagram. Other tools available in quality management include flowcharts, experimental design, failure modes, and effects analysis (FMEA); conjoint analysis; poka-yoke; the Taguchi method; quality function deployment (QFD); statistical process control (SPC); and the quality circle.

A study by Lagrosen and Lagrosen (2005) found that the most common method used is the flow diagram method (60.8%), followed by FMEA (39%) and seven quality control tools (29.4%). Other tools based on the user include SPC (29.4%), the quality circle (17.0%), experimental design (16.2%), QFD (12.8%), seven management tools (11.3%), poka-yoke (7.2%), the Taguchi method (3.4%), and conjoint analysis (1.1%).

The study by Lagrosen and Lagrosen (2005) also revealed that, in general, TQM has imperfect effectiveness in achieving goals. In studies on 500 members of the Association of Swedish Quality, 8.3% of them use Six Sigma as the quality improvement method, while the rest use the TQM method or others (ISO 9000, QS 9000, Swedish Quality Award, European Quality Award, and Malcolm Beldrige National Quality Award). This revealed that 15.8% of the respondents did not find any positive effect. This means that 84.2% had positive effects. These positive effects include improvements to processes (46.8%); increased participation (12.8%); improved climate, including the understanding of quality and a more holistic view (12.5%); and improvement in the customer aspects such as customer satisfaction, market share, and so on (12.1%). Still,

15.8% of the implementations of quality improvement methods reflect that the elephant analogy above still applies. We have not really found the right method to improve quality as much as possible without any gaps that come from imperfection of the implementation or organizational external interference.

Furthermore, in addition to still needing to complete the TQM model, we still have to improve the practices or conceptions that already exist. Lagrosen and Lagrosen's study (2005) also found a negative effect of TQM in 42.6% of the projects. That is, almost half of the TQM projects undertaken will create special problems that need to be addressed as soon as TQM makes them appear. These problems include increased workload (19.1%), increased bureaucracy (16.7%), and focus branching (6.8%).

References

Andersson, R., H. Eriksson, and H. Torstensson. 2006. Similarities and differences between TQM, Six Sigma and Lean. *TQM Magazine* 18(3), 282–296.

Lagrosen, Y. and S. Lagrosen. 2005. The effects of quality management—A survey of Swedish quality professionals. *International Journal of Operations & Production Management* 25(10), 940–952.

Moen, R. and C. Norman. 2006. Evolution of the PDCA cycle.

Chapter 12

Lean Implementation in Hospitals

Introduction

One of the most popular methods to improve quality in hospitals is Lean. Lean is chosen because it is more specific than TQM and Six Sigma, but on the other hand, it is better able to deliver results because it is systematic and deals directly with the problem of waste. Waste is "an activity or behavior that adds the cost but do not add value as perceived by the end customer" (Emiliani, 2006: 3). Lean can be strategic and focus on the principles and culture of the organization for long-term results, and it can be operational, namely in the application of tools and techniques. Implementation in the scope of health services shows that Lean is able to speed up the way to get care services, cost reduction, increased productivity, error reduction, and increases of staff and patient satisfaction (Aguilar-Escobar et al., 2015: 102).

Waste

One form of inefficiency is waste of turnover of goods. Turnover of goods in large hospitals is a serious issue because it deals with wait time. In the context of an emergency, it can cost one's life. Physicians alone might experience stress due to the responsibilities imposed on them related to the problem of goods. Furfari (2009: 22) cited cases where physicians have to move to a different floor to examine a patient. Additionally, an ambulance can be useless when it is in another place when needed. Overall, Table 12.1 shows the various types of waste in hospitals.

Lean Implementation

Lean implementation in the hospital became more important in the Universal Health Coverage era when there was a surge of patient visits (Rachmat, 2014). There have been many hospitals in Indonesia that have implemented Lean methods to improve quality. The concept was developed in 2010 at Cipto Mangunkusumo Hospital in Indonesia in building A, which has 900 beds. Lean has implemented in Sumber Waras Hospital Ciwaringin in Indonesia in 2015, for example, because its wait time was too long. It was identified that 90% of service time does not add value, and, through Lean, activities that do not add value have been reduced to only 70.59% (Tjahjanto, 2016). The same was done by Pelni Hospital, which tried some tools such as Kaizen (continuous improvement), Kanban (just in time), and Genchi Genbutsu (blusukan) (Alomet et al., 2015).

Lean methods were developed at Toyota in 1950 by Taichi Ohno. In its initial form, Lean was referred to as the Toyota Production System (TPS). It was used to drive Toyota into a major manufacturing company in the world and was soon adopted by many other companies in manufacturing and finally in the field of health care.

When compared to Lean manufacturing, the use of Lean in hospitals is most oriented to timeliness or waste of time (Cahyono, 2008). Lean manufacturing is more oriented toward the production aspects (production waste). In Lean

Table 12.1 Various Types of Waste in Hospitals

Type of Waste	Example
Overproduction waste	• Fragmented social services, including companions, interns, and patients' service cycle • Entering information repeatedly on various documents or forms
Waste of time	• Primary team waiting for supporting services • Patients waiting for further agreements • Delay in giving a patient a bed
Waste of product transport	• Primary team walks to a different floor to see the patient • Waiting for transport to arrive, taking patients to be examined, procedure/surgery, released
Waste through excessive processes	• Many computer programs for documenting patient care information • Ordering more diagnostic tests than needed to guarantee a diagnosis • Retesting
Waste of supplies	• Drugs and duplicate supplies exceed normal use • Unnecessary instruments in the operating room equipment • Diagrams, files, tools, and papers that have expired
Waste of movement	• Nurses leave the patient's room for general supplies • Looking for diagrams, patients, drugs
Waste in making errors	• Iatrogenic diseases • Medical errors

Source: Furfari, K. 2009. The Lean Hospital: What Does It Mean? University of Colorado Hospital [online], http://www.uch.edu, accessed September 9, 2013.

manufacturing, the problem of time is not as significant because production has been standardized and scheduled well so that the main issue is to lower production costs. In a Lean hospital, production is not very standardized (each patient can have a different complaint), and the time standard is difficult to predict (the service time of one patient is different from that of other patients). As a result, the problem of time becomes a very important issue. Therefore, the Lean hospital adds a time dimension that is less often explored in Lean manufacturing.

Lean Principles

Lean principles can be broadly summarized as follows in Figure 12.1. In this figure, the quality of the hospital system is comparable to a building. The roof of the building is the main objective, namely improving the health care system of the hospital. It is supported by two pillars, namely just in time (JIT) and quality. JIT is an effort to work with the minimum resources needed to proceed. JIT contains four principles, namely only do what it takes, only do the appropriate amount requested, only provided as needed, and only work when needed. In Japanese, JIT is operationalized in the form of

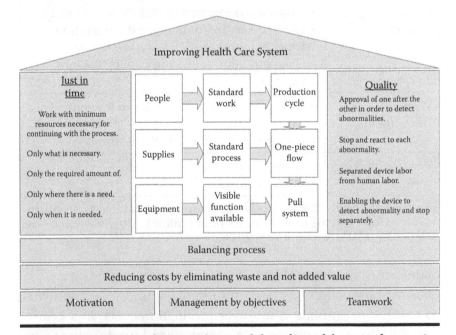

Figure 12.1 Lean implementation model. (Adapted from Kadarova, J. and M. Demecko. 2016. *Procedia Economics and Finance* 39, 11–16.)

Kanban (sign card). Kanban is a system that allows management of the entire supply chain by linking production requests strategically and operationally with supply management. Kanban creates material flow involving employees to control and improve the processes between work stations. It works by generating/delivering the expected components only when necessary. This is achieved by a visual signal in the form of cards, boxes, or empty containers. In turn, Kanban reduces costs not only by eliminating waste, but also by being more responsive to change; facilitating quality control; and providing important roles, trust, and support to the employees who carry out the processes (Aguillor-Escobar et al., 2015: 102).

The second pillar, quality, contains four principles: receive one by one pieces to detect abnormalities, stop and react to any abnormality, separate the work of man and machine, and allow tools to detect abnormalities and stop separately. Both pillars are then supported by two layers of flooring, namely balancing processes and cost reduction by removing waste and activities that do not add value. Waste and activities that do not add value economically contribute, on average, 40% of total health care costs. Waste can be in the form of time; supplies; materials; medication; information; food; unnecessary procedures; wrong medications; delayed treatment; misdiagnosis; failure to meet good work requirements; lack of communication; chaos at work; a long wait time to get materials, tools, personnel, and related matters; bad disposition of materials and tools; workspaces that are not well ordered; waste of energy; too many reserves; unnecessary and long meetings; and drug and medical supply expiration (Kadarova and Demecko, 2016: 13).

Finally, the floor is supported by three foundations: motivation, objective-based management, and teamwork. The leadership role is important as a foundation for enabling these three things. The often-used method is called Genchi Genbutsu or go-to-Gemba. This principle asks the superior to go downstairs (to the front office) on a regular basis to fully understand the ongoing processes, thus allowing for correct decision making. The most practical tool from Genchi Genbutsu is the Ohno circle, an imaginary or even real circle drawn on the floor. The leader then enters the circle to observe the process. This activity may take several hours until the leader really understands the process, including failures and the possibilities for fixing them (Dombrowski and Mielke, 2013: 571).

Within this house, the Lean process works by targeting humans, supplies, and equipment. Humans are encouraged through standardized work to promote the production cycle, which is continuously monitored through the value stream mapping (VSM) method, the supply is promoted through standardization of processes to produce flow one by one, and the equipment is promoted by the 5S method.

Supplies and equipment are monitored by the 5S method (Sort—remove what is not needed, Straighten—organize what is left, Shine—clean the workspace, Standardize—schedule periodic cleaning and maintenance, and Sustain—make 5S as a way of life).

Visual management is intended to determine the errors that occur in health care using Lean (de Koning et al., 2006). This happens because visual management allows the staff to view the status at any time on the system and find out if there is a problem in the system (Fillingham, 2007). The staff can immediately make improvements in the process that has the problem. Visual management can be run after the 5S method. After the workspace is neat, visual management will continue to inspect the workspace and the work going on in it in a sustainable manner. Visual management can be run at any time if you want the setup of working space better. The visual management system enables the system to work through the pull system, which is also promoted by flowing one by one.

Empirically, the five main Lean tools (5S, VSM, visual management, standardized work, and pull systems) have been known to provide benefits to patients as well as hospitals and insurance companies/BPJS health. Table 12.2 summarizes the

Table 12.2 Lean Benefits in Hospitals

Methods	Benefits for Patients	Benefits for Hospital and Insurance Company
5S	Quick service, reduce wait time	Increase productivity, reduce costs, and space
VSM	Shorten time, eliminate waste, improve diagnosis and treatment	Reduce downtime, operational, and personnel costs and get happier customers
Visual management	Reduce personnel errors, improve patient orientation, improve quality of patient service	Reduce diagnosis and treatment errors, clarify and simplify; staff move faster
Standardized work	Reduce the risk of human error	Reduce the risk of human error, increase productivity and control
Pull system	Faster treatment, increase the availability of key tasks, reduce queues	Reduce inventory, improve the capacity of workspace utilization, reduce unnecessary requests

benefits of the implementation of the five main Lean methods individually within the framework of the Lean principles of a hospital.

The final stage of lean is Kaizen. Kaizen is done to create excellence and continuous improvement. The form used to be known as A3. The form contains reasons to make improvements. Current conditions and expected ideal conditions as future conditions. Then, action/improvement measures are taken to move toward the desired condition. Last is the success indicator of the remedial measures that have been implemented. More details can be seen in Figure 12.2.

Continuous improvement measures are carried out by strengthening teams, routine audits, and the communication of achievement of the results through a visual board (dashboard).

Lean Project Board/Kaizen

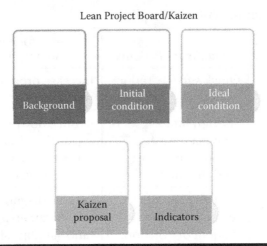

Figure 12.2   Kaizen.

There are two types of improvement carried out, namely, the "Kaizen individual" and the "Kaizen team." Individual kaizen means individuals who are informal making small improvements with a daily duration, while a Kaizen team is more formal and its focus is larger. This activity is carried out by implementing the PDCA cycle, since it is easy and familiar. At the Plan stage, the team creates a plan and improvement ideas that will be developed based on the identified issues. Do consists of doing experiments on the ideas that have been determined at the Plan stage. Then, Check analyzes the data by assessing/evaluating the results of the improvements that have been carried out and compared to the target. The final step is Act, where teams select the best activities that give optimal results using minimal resources.

References

Aguilar-Escobar, V. G., S. Bourque, and N. Godino-Gallego. 2015. Hospital Kanban system implementation: Evaluating satisfaction of nursing personnel. *Investigaciones Europeas de Dirección y Economía de la Empresa* 21(3), 101–110.

Alomet & Friends. November 12, 2015. Implementation of Lean management di Pelni Hospital start reaping results and benefits. [online], available: http://www.kompasiana.com/alomet/penerapan-lean-management-di-rs-pelni-mulai-menuai-hasil-manfaat_564411a2b 69373240551dfa4. (Accessed December 9, 2016.)

Cahyono, J. B. and B. Suharjo. 2008. Membangun budaya keselamatan pasien dalam praktik kedokteran, Kanisius, Yogyakarta.

De Koning, H., J. P. S. Verver, J. Van den Heuvel, S. Bisgaard, and R. J. M. M. Does. 2006. Lean Six Sigma in healthcare. *Journal for Healthcare Quality* 28(2), 4–11.

Dombrowski, U. and T. Mielke. 2013. Lean leadership—Fundamental principles and their application. *Procedia CIRP* 7, 569–574.

Emiliani, M. L. 2004. Improving business school courses by applying lean principles and practices. *Quality Assurance in Education* 12(4), 175–187.

Fillingham, D. 2007. Can Lean save lives? *Leadership in Health Services* 20(4), 231–241.

Furfari, K. 2009. The Lean hospital: What does it mean? University of Colorado Hospital [online], available: http://www.uch.edu. (Accessed September 9, 2013.)

Kadarova, J. and M. Demecko. 2016. New approaches in Lean management. *Procedia Economics and Finance* 39, 11–16.

Rachmat, F. D. September 30, 2014. Patient safety in the operating room using quality perspective compass. https://fathemadjan.wordpress.com/2014/09/30/keselamatan-pasien-di-kamar-operasi/.

Tjahjanto, A. 2016. Lean thinking methods to improve the efficiency of outpatient services in Sumber Waras Hospital Ciwaringin in 2015. Thesis. University of Indonesia, Jakarta, Indonesia.

Chapter 13

Utilization of Hospital Resources

Introduction

Hospital resources have to come from external sources, which will allow the hospital to live and develop. The cost for these resources is raised from various sources, but the sustainable source for public hospitals is the government itself, through the budget. Meanwhile, the capital cost for private hospitals must come from investors. Most of these sources cover only the capital cost, while operating costs must be covered by other sources. The source is the patient, who in turn can be self-financed or financed by insurance, including BPJS.

When faced with a situation of illness or symptoms of illness, an individual does not directly choose the hospital to eliminate the health problems. There are many considerations. Some of these considerations include (Zweifel and Manning, 2000: 412):

1. The scope of the health insurance coverage owned
2. What disease prevention efforts should be carried out before giving up
3. Whether to get health care

4. The choice of formal or traditional/alternative health care
5. Whether to seek treatment at home or in a hospital
6. Whether to contact private or public health care
7. The choice of which health care to use

When there is a change in the patient's ability to pay the hospital or changes in the insurance scheme, it will have an impact on the price of hospital services provided to patients. This is because the patients provide the demand, and the hospital is the party that gives the supply. If demand changes, in the end, the supply also changes. Internally, changes also occur in the efficiency and equity of hospital services. If the hospital rates rise, there is a possibility that the hospital will experience a change in efficiency due to changes in demand. Similarly, a hospital rate increase will make some level of society unable to afford the cost; therefore, the equality of service will decrease.

A concept that is relevant to hospital demand is elasticity. Elasticity shows changes in the quantity of goods or services requested along with price changes. If the consumer demand for hospital services is very elastic, then small changes in hospital rates will result in a major decline in demand, and, consequently, the hospital will see only a little profit over the rate increase. Conversely, if consumer demand is inelastic (rigid), then changes in demand will be smaller than changes in the price of hospital services. The hospital can raise prices, and the number of requests will not change much, so the hospital can earn substantial profits, or, if it has losses, the losses will be small.

Elasticity of demand can be seen from the contribution margin. A high contribution margin reflects low elasticity of demand. CM, contribution margin, is defined as (Gaynor et al., 2013: 254):

$$CM = \frac{p - c}{p}$$

where p is the price, and c is the unit cost. That is, the contribution margin is the ratio between profit and costs. A very high contribution margin means that the company is very profitable, and it certainly reflects that the demand is not elastic, so there is not much change even if the hospital raises prices. However, the hospital is not able to raise prices as high as possible because patients can transfer to another hospital that offers a lower rate. As a result, the profit from the contribution margin is the greatest in situations of monopoly or cartel. Even in a situation like this, patients can still go somewhere else if a hospital in another place (e.g., in another city or country) provides cheap rates and travel costs as well as travel risks that patients are still able to handle rather than having to pay higher rates.

Next, we need to take a look at consumer use of hospitals. Utilization (utility) U, consumer i, and a number of hospitals j has the form of (Gaynor et al., 2013: 256):

$$U_{ij} = -\alpha_p p_j - p_j X_{ij}^p \alpha + X_{ij}\beta + X_j\gamma + \xi_j + \varepsilon_{ij}$$

where p_j is a hospital fare; α_p is the utilization of marginal revenue; X is the observable characteristics of consumers, hospitals, and their interactions; X^p is the consumer interaction characteristics and hospitals with the price; and ε_j is hospital characteristics that are not observed. Consumers will choose a hospital that provides the highest utility for them.

Consumer Rates

As explained earlier, consumer rates are related to the elasticity of demand. If the demand is elastic, tariff changes would result in large changes in the consumer demand. Conversely, if the demand is not elastic, tariff changes do not result in major changes in consumer demand. This is illustrated in Figure 13.1.

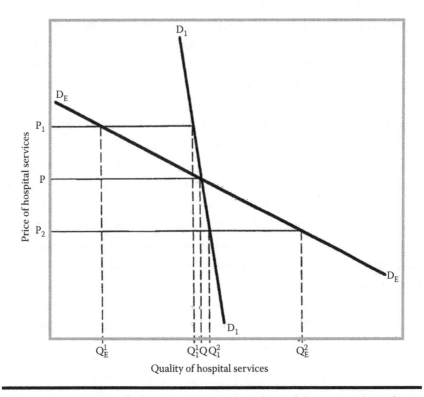

Figure 13.1   Demand elasticity hospital. (Adapted from Newbrander, W., H. Barnum, and J. Kutzin. 1992. *Hospital Economics and Financing in Developing Countries*. Geneva: World Health Organization.)

In Figure 13.1, the DE demand curve is the elastic demand, and DI is inelastic. The point of intersection between the two curves is the equilibrium point, which indicates the equilibrium price P and quantity supplied Q. In a situation of inelasticity (DI), the increase in price from P to P1 will generate very little shift from Q to QI1. But if demand is elastic (DE), the shift from P to P1 will result in a major shift from Q to QE1. Conversely, if the price is lowered from P to P2, the quantity consumed by patients will rise from Q to QE2 on the elastic curve (DE). This change is great when compared to the price reduction from P to P2, which results in only a small increase in demand from Q to QI2.

In 17 countries in Africa, the government fully funds health services for the community. The government even provides penalties for hospitals that request rates from patients (Leighton, 1996: 1518). Meanwhile, in a situation where the government guarantees free health care on the part of the community, especially the poor, the amount of consumption of health services in high-income communities actually increased compared to the poor. This is because the upper classes perceive that if they pay for themselves, they get better service, which encourages them to consume more hospital services than they should (Sepehri et al., 2005).

Insurance

Finance-based health insurance is complex because the incentives due to insurance occur on both the supply and demand sides. If the patient is paid entirely by insurance, he or she may ask for more services and higher quality than he or she should at the hospital, compared to when the patient pays in part or fully. The hospital will also be happy because it earns a higher income and can even take steps that increase the income, for example, by not providing enough prescription drugs at a time to health patients so that the patients have to come to the hospital regularly, or by bringing more patients to the operating room or outpatient emergency than usual in order to get more money from the insurance company. This has occurred because of human behavior that wants to get the maximum profit and is hence termed a moral hazard (Newbrander et al., 1992: 27).

According to the theory of moral hazard, insurance agents will try to avoid risk in order to keep from paying, while the patients covered do not have orientation on certain risks (neutral) but are still paying a premium to the insurance agents. This provides the optimum situation from the standpoint of risk sharing when the company pays the entire cost when the risk occurs. However, because patients are neutral, they do not have the desire to reduce the risk unless given an incentive.

Therefore, patients should be given a portion of the existing risk in order to derive personal benefits from avoiding the risk; for example, consider the incidence of traffic accidents. Because he or she is insured, a person is not too concerned if a traffic accident happens and does not feel the need to take steps to reduce the risk because he/she has paid the insurance premium regularly. Because of this lack of worry, individuals can get involved in situations that invite the risk of accidents more often than if they are not insured. As a result, the risks faced by the insurer are greater. To keep customers from engaging in risky behavior, the customer must be given partial responsibility for paying medical expenses (Chiappori et al., 1998: 501).

The insurance business generally issues three types of mechanisms to prevent moral catastrophes of the part of patients and hospitals: deductible, copayments, and coverage limits (Newbrander et al., 1992: 27). The deductible system asks patients to pay for their own health care up to a limit. Once this limit is passed, the insurer will pay the rest. The problem is to determine the limit for the patient payment. If this limit is too low, the moral hazard problem still occurs because patients pay a little money to get the maximum service. If it is too high, the insurance business loses its appeal to the public, and if the insurance is run by the government, such as through BPJS, it may prevent the community from getting universal and equal health services.

The copayment mechanism asks the patients to pay a certain percentage of the total cost. This mechanism is seen to be fair but is very difficult to implement. The difficulty comes from the efficiency problem. Imagine a hospital bill is divided by two parties, although the cost of the bill is only IDR20,000. For example, the patients pay 10% of the cost, meaning the patients must include money IDR2000 plus the insurance card. Similarly, if the patient has to pay 90%, the insurance company must pay IDR2000, which is certainly not efficient because the value is too low, perhaps even more than the cost of administrative arrangements. Consequently, the copayment scheme is efficient only if the hospital cost is quite large. But this still does not completely remove the moral hazard because patients pay less for expensive services.

The third mechanism, the coverage limit, asks the patient to pay in advance up to a maximum limit. Once this limit is exceeded, the insurance covers all payments. This kind of insurance is suitable for long-term illness. For instance, if the coverage limit is IDR9 million, the patient will continue to pay for health care up to IDR9 million. Afterward, the costs will be covered by the insurance. This is considered the best, but it still reduces the attractiveness of insurance, with the same problem as the deductible problem.

In the end, insurance programs must be designed with caution, taking into account factors such as the probability of occurrence of disease, consumers' taste, the amount of funds covered, the type of dependents, and underwriting methods.

References

Chiappori, P.-A., D. Franck, and G. Pierre-Yves. 1998. Moral hazard and the demand for physician services: First lessons from a French natural experiment. *European Economic Review* 42(3), 499–511.

Gaynor, M. S., S. A. Kleiner, and W. B. Vogt. 2013. A structural approach to market definition with an application to the hospital industry. *Journal of Industrial Economics* 61(2), 243–289.

Leighton, C. 1996. Strategies for achieving health financing reform in Africa. *World Development* 24(9), 1511–1525.

Newbrander, W., H. Barnum, and J. Kutzin. 1992. *Hospital Economics and Financing in Developing Countries*, Geneva: World Health Organization.

Sepehri, A., R. Chernomas, and H. Akram-Lodhi. 2005. Penalizing patients and rewarding providers: User charges and health care utilization in Vietnam. *Health Policy and Planning* 20(2), 90–99.

Zweifel, P. and W. G. Manning. 2000. Moral hazard and consumer incentives in health care. *Handbook of Health Economics* 1, 409–459.

Chapter 14

Hospital Revenue Components

Introduction

Previously, it has been mentioned that hospital revenue components basically consist of two kinds: tariffs of patients and insurance (public or private). Before BPJS is applied on a national scale, there are 14 ways to pay hospital costs. These include:

1. *Private*. Patients pay their medical costs independently or are assisted by an insurance company to which patients pay a premium.
2. *SHI (Social Health Insurance)*. A payment made by the participants who are included as a worker community in the formal sector through the insurance system.
3. *Company Assurance*. A payment that is totally borne by the company.
4. *NHI (National Health Insurance)*. A payment made by the state for civil servants.

5. *CHI (Community Health Insurance)*. A payment made by the state for the poor and incapable.

6. *Childbirth Assurance*. A payment of delivery funding starting from gestation examination, delivery assistance, childbed services, postdelivery family planning services, and newborn services provided by the state for society.

7. *LHI (Local Government Health Insurance)*. A payment made by the local government for the poor and low-income community. Depending on the local government, LHI is less used due to difficulties in billing (Supriyantoro, 2013: 3).

8. *Poor Family/OT*. A payment made by the government for poor families and displaced people.

9. *Subsidies*. Cost subtraction for patients for various reasonable excuses.

10. *Free of charge*. A total cost exemption for patients; it is generally because the patient is an employee of the hospital.

11. *PC (Poverty Certificate)*. A payment made by the government for a family that owns a poverty letter. PC is the most acceptable payment in emergency department services when patients cannot prove membership in CHI/LHI.

12. *Extraordinary Cases*. A payment made by the government for those who experience an extraordinary event. This type of payment occurs only in the case of widespread epidemic disease.

13. *Health Service Guarantee*. A payment made by the government for the families of the workforce. Health Service Guarantee is applicable only for pharmaceutical prescriptions.

14. *MCUs (Medical Check-Ups)*. A payment made by an organization for its employees who take regular medical checks. MCU is a payment model that may be applied for laboratory installations.

Payment-Based System

There are two kinds of payments based on time (Bastian, 2008):

1. *Prospective payment*, which is a health service with assurance (indirect payment). A prospective payment is made to fund an agreement and further made before the provision or service is performed, no matter how much the actual cost spent by the hospital, such as through a fixed payment per individual per time unit.
2. *Retrospective payment*, which is an agreed-upon payment made after the service is performed. Retrospective payment is payment per item (free for service) because patients pay the full cost to the hospital after the service, such as after diagnosis action, pharmacy, therapy, and so on.

The following is an example of an annual revenue report from Penyakit Infeksi Prof dr Sulianti Saroso Jakarta Hospital in 2013. Based on the data, it can be seen that the number of patients who paid by the general method was one-third of the total number of patients, while 46% used the LHI facility and 15% NHI, 2% SHI, 1% Poor family/OT, and 1% were free of charge. The proportion of patients for each installation is significantly different. The highest number of public patients were in the emergency department, at 82%, while the intensive care unit had only 8% of public patients. There were many patients in the intensive care unit who used LHI for the payment method (66%). On the contrary, only 3% of patients in the emergency department used the LHI facility. In the era of BPJS, society should continue to pay the cost for emergency department services by themselves (Daniel, 2016).

Hospital Revenue

Hospital revenue may be from sources other than the medical installations discussed above. Other sources of hospital revenue come from both nonmedical revenue centers such as funeral homes, parking lots, cafeterias, auditoriums, training, incinerators (medical waste burners), and WWTPs (wastewater treatment plants) and medical revenue centers such as drug-stores and ambulances (Table 14.1). Generally, these revenues are categorized as revenues from cooperation with a third party, wealth utilization, grant revenue, or other legal revenue using wealth potential.

The existence of BPJS allows the number of BPJS patients to reach 70% of the total patients in the hospital. Public patients partly become BPJS patients due to affordable premi-ums with certain insurances in medical funding (Isa, 2015). By this scheme, the profit of the public hospital remains about 10%, while the profit of private hospitals reaches 20% (Protes Publik, 2015). However, because BPJS is progressive, by the time the number of BPJS patients increases, the proportion of BPJS patients is getting bigger as well. In addition, incoming INA-CBG claims are higher compared to the previous year with the same number of cases which indicates there is an increase in hospital revenue.

On the other hand, there are two groups of hospitals that do not cooperate with BPJS Kesehatan. The first group is premium hospitals, which are not affected because they serve patients who do not mind the cost. The second group is hos-pitals with middle-to-lower-class patients, which have experi-enced a decrease in visits. These hospitals should cooperate with BPJS K to attract patients like before. However, revenue reduction has continued to occur for some time due to a delay by BPJS K because of a full quota. In January 2016, the per-centage of hospitals that have become partners of BPJS was 70.23% (1729 of 2462) of the available hospitals in Indonesia.

The point is that hospitals gain many patients due to the existence of BPJS, particularly for hospitals that cooperate with BPJS. This affects the increase of hospital revenue because, although the profit margin from BPJS is low, the greater num-ber of patients beats having very few patients and a high

Table 14.1 Examples of Hospital Revenue Source Proportions before BPJS

	Private (%)	SHI (%)	Company Assurance (%)	NHI (%)	Childbirth Assurance (%)	LHI (%)	Poor Family/ OT (%)	Free of Charge (%)
Inpatients	28	2	1	8	1	60	0	0
Outpatients	54	1	0	17	0	28	0	0
ICU	8	4	0	20	0	66	0	0
ED	82	3	0	7	0	3	3	0
Pharmaceutical Prescription	25	1	0	7	0	58	0	
Laboratory	32	2	0	15	0	48	1	7
Radiology	45	1	0	14	0	39	1	0
Medical Rehab	20	1	0	36	0	42	0	0
Surgery	11	2	0	16	2	69	0	0
Average	34	2	0	15	0	46	1	1

Source: Daniel. 2016. *Harapan—Kenyataan dan Solusi JKN Perspektif PERSI.* Jakarta: PERSI.

profit margin. There are some variations, in which there are hospitals experiencing a drastic increase in service while other hospitals still complain about unearned costs. The unearned costs of this claim are because there is no agreement on case resolution, so claims are late. This disturbs hospital cash flow. Some hospitals even experience a decrease in revenue due to changes in the composition of public patients.

However, there are some problems encountered by hospitals in the BPJS system. These problems include (Daniel, 2016):

1. Particularly for hospitals in big cities, it is not optimum to manage patient diagnoses due to the too-great demand. This results in a decrease of clinical service quality. With BPJS, hospitals are capable of growing without sacrificing service quality or health professionalism, and the hospital and society obtain adequate returns.

2. Grouping and the amount of INA-CBG rates are considered unrealistic, especially for hospitals with high base levels. This is also an issue for the Ministry of Health for the purpose of adjusting particular diagnosis groups and actions in INA-CBG and rate regionalization that has not been in accordance with hospital service unit cost. The existence of too much of an INA-CBG tariff difference among hospitals, which should be based only on competence or facility and infrastructure availability, becomes a factor that causes referrals among hospitals. Referring to one another, in addition to the basic problem of referrals in hospitals, is not in accordance with hospital competence, so the gradual referring system is weakening each hospital. This is used by hospitals to conduct case sorting in accordance with diagnostics based on payment rates rather than competence. This kind of sorting allows hospitals to obtain more revenue, especially from middle-class patients.

3. There is still a misunderstanding of diagnosis coding and visit episodes between hospitals and BPJS K. This

is indicated by numerous reports of hospitals that feel aggrieved by the perception of verifiers and BPJS K in interpreting diagnoses into diagnosis codes (PERSI, 2016).

4. The provision of charging premiums and coordination of benefits (CoB) remains unclear.
5. BPJS K is considered a monopoly, so it affects regulation.
6. Some nonregional public service board (RPSB) regional hospital doctors think that their income does not fit with their workload. In addition, in non-RPSB hospitals, there is an obstacle to medicine, structure, and facility provision due to a lack of understanding of rational medicine necessity on the part of the Regent and Regional House of Representatives.
7. There are perception differences in the matter of fraud between hospitals and BPJS K.
8. Price differences exist in medicine acquisition for nongovernment hospitals due to obstacles in purchasing with the e-catalog tariff.
9. There is no facility-standard system for treatment class of hospitals.

In addition, hospitals are still unable to face BPJS because some hospitals still employ free for service (FFS)-based services and do not possess a list of the competencies of the hospital and its level, which causes hospital classification that does not reflect 100% of the hospital competence, and hospital service quality standardization is still varied, so there are still many hospitals that do not have the courage to ask for accreditation. Also, there is conflict between management and doctors who feel that their right to make clinical decisions is limited, and there are obstacles in satisfying health professionals' HR (PERSI, 2016).

Meanwhile, the hospital market is still dominated by a claim ratio imbalance between independent and nonindependent groups. Independent groups consist of nonwage workers (NWWs) and nonworkers (NWs), who amounted to only 12 million people but possess utility up to 85%, and many of them suffer from catastrophe. Meanwhile, nonindependent groups consist of premiums for aid recipients and wage workers and possess utility up to only 5% (PERSI, 2016).

BPJS Kesehatan would clearly evolve in the future to meet the needs of all parties. Therefore, IHA (Indonesian Hospital Association) advises several important improvements related to justice for hospitals. Some of these improvements include (PERSI, 2016):

1. Hospital class should be standardized on the basis of minimal clinical competence, which is supported by facilities and HR and referenced as the basis of competence mapping of the available hospitals.
2. INA-CBG tariffs should accommodate the HR wage index, obstacles in disposable medical instrument supply, cases with relatively high cost, and incentives for private hospitals, as well as reasonable case weights for outpatients and inpatients, so it is not only limited to budget adequacy.
3. Hospitals should divide claims into a basic claim paid by BPJS K and a premium claim (top up) paid by health insurance with the prospective method, except for the VIP class, which uses the retrospective method. This would increase hospital "happiness" because it creates the opportunity for premium tariff negotiation with health insurance.
4. There should be a credential process of BPJS K partner hospitals involving the Health Department and PERSI.
5. For some areas in Indonesia, it is possible that payment for hospitals could use a budget system due to lack of administrative and clinical resources.
6. Tax incentives are needed for hospitals that are BPJS participants, as well as hospital accounting standardization for financial system–based financial management for funding from JKN so it can accommodate prospective payments in large portions.

References

Bastian, I. 2008. *Akuntansi Kesehatan.* First Edition. Jakarta: Erlangga.

Daniel. 2016. *Harapan—Kenyataan dan Solusi JKN Perspektif PERSI.* Jakarta: PERSI.

Isa, M. 2015. BPJS—Banyak Pasien Jadi Senang! http://bpjs-kesehatan.go.id/bpjs/index.php/post/read/2015/366/BPJS-Banyak-Pasien-Jadi-Senang.

PERSI. 2016. *Refleksi Dua Tahun JKN.* Jakarta: PERSI, hal. 3.

Protes Publik. 2015. BPJS Kesehatan Dongkrak Omzet Rumah Sakit. http://protespublik.com/detail/post/31/BPJS-Kesehatan-Dongkrak-Omzet-Rumah-Sakit. (Accessed December 21, 2017.)

Supriyantoro. 2013. *Formulasi Kebijakan Integrasi Jaminan Kesehatan Daerah ke Sistem Jaminan Kesehatan Nasional Menuju Universal Health Coverage, Disertasi.* Jogjakarta, Indonesia: UGM.

Chapter 15

Diagnosis-Related Groups

Introduction

Hospital economical control related to effectiveness and productivity needs an independent framework against specialization in the hospital. An independent character is important because by being free from specialization, resource allocation can be performed well, especially in the case where some specializations are competing with each other (Ninimaki et al., 1991: 41). This is satisfied through diagnosis-related groups (DRGs). The main purpose of DRGs is to determine the type of case that is expected to obtain a similar output or service from certain hospitals.

DRGs contain important data with input in the form of diagnosis, surgery, age, other complications, length of stay, and particular costs (Ninimaki et al., 1991: 40). In line with the importance of these data, a DRG is none other than complications from various diagnosis groups that determine diagnostic and therapeutic consumption from hospital resources on each group. It is a patient classification scheme that relates demography, diagnosis, and therapy of patients to hospital resource consumption.

DRGs are used as a patient classification system for hospital cost analysis. However, some critics have claimed DRGs are related to quite large internal variations in comorbidity, a lack of sensibility in various medical practices used in similar diseases, and diagnosis and therapy procedure indications that are not always totally evaluated (Rodriguez-Rieiro et al., 2012: 444). Other critics state that some relevant clinical variables are not recorded even though they should be considered, like the level of disease severity. The use of DRG data for hospital cost analysis should consider the matter of administrative recoding, which is probably biased as well, so the data used should have been audited and validated.

DRGs were initially implemented in the United States as a return system for hospitals. The initial version of DRGs was implemented in 1977 and consisted of 383 diagnosis groups, which were then developed into 492 groups. Various countries then implemented DRGs at different times. In Germany, DRGs have been used for operational cost funding of hospital services since 2010 (Kriegel et al., 2016: 4). Table 15.1 shows some DRG variations.

Theoretically, DRGs are the medium for payment mechanisms in health system organizations. The simpler form of DRGs is Fee For Services (FFS), which considers only cost based on the patient's visit. Meanwhile, the most complex form of DRGs is patient global payment per enrollee. DRGs are not suitable to be implemented at doctors' practices, clinics for outpatients, or basic health service practices. It begins to be effective when it is implemented in an integrated hospital system and health service system. Figure 15.1 shows the relationship between the available types of payment mechanism and type of health system organization.

Diagnosis-Related Groups in Indonesia

The implementation of DRGs in Indonesia (INA-DRG) was started in 2007 through a Decree of the Indonesia Minister of

Table 15.1 Types of DRGs

Name	The Number of Groups	Explanation
Medicare Diagnosis Related Group (Medicare-DRG)	492	The second modification of initial version of DRGs; it only includes elderly patients (>65 years old)
All Patients DRG (AP-DRG)	641	Medicare-DRG is added with neonates, pediatric disease, and HIV infection groups
International Refined DRG (IR-DRG)	965	It corresponds to variations of local clinical conditions
Refined DRG	1170	It uses LOS in grouping, modification of secondary diagnosis
All Patient Refined DRG (APR-DRG)	1530	It consists more of neonates, pediatric, HIV infections, multiple traumatic medical care, and other diseases

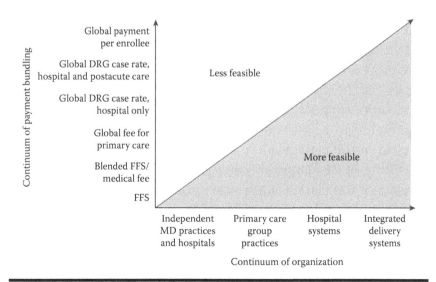

Figure 15.1   Mechanisms of payment and health service organization. (Adapted from Rokx, C. et al. 2009. *Health Financing in Indonesia: A Reform Road Map.* **Washington, DC: World Bank Publications, 104.)**

Health No. 1161/Menkes/SK/X/2007 on Decision of Hospital Rates Based on Indonesia Diagnosis Related Group (INA-DRG). Previously, this system was tried at 15 hospitals as a calculation system of service costs through the Decree of Indonesia Minister of Health No. 1663/Menkes/SK/XII/2005 on Implementation Experiment of Case-Mix Diagnosis Related Group (DRG) System. The rationale for DRG implementation in Indonesia is that it provides tariff and transparent standardization, more objective tariff calculation on the basis of the actual cost, hospital payments that are based on the actual work load, and the ability to increase hospital service quality and efficiency.

There are 1077 disease groups, with 23 categories of main diagnoses. This number is considered large for a developing country. Generally, developing countries have DRGs consisting of 500–800 groups. In Kyrgyzstan and Mongolia, the number of groups is lower. Meanwhile, in Thailand, there are 2700 case groups. The high number of cases encompassed in the DRGs indicates that the available health system service is quite advanced, so it is able to provide various services (Mathauer and Wittenbecher, 2013).

INA-DRG was derived from IR-DRG by adding several new groups based on characteristics of Indonesia. INA-DRG consists of 789 inpatient DRGs and 288 outpatient DRGs. The main supporting data to determine INA-DRG codes were obtained from ICD-10 and ICD-9 CM. ICD-10 is the tenth revision of the classification system of international disease consisting of 21 diagnostic categories. ICD-9 CM is the ninth revision of the classification system of international disease with clinically necessity modifications consisting of 16 diagnostic categories. The government buys INA-DRG licenses for Rp 4 billion, and this license ended on September 30, 2010. The main diagnostic categories of INA-DRG include:

1. Disease and nervous system disorders
2. Disease and eye disorders

3. Disease and ear, nasal, oral, and larynx disorders
4. Disease and respiratory system disorders
5. Disease and circulatory system disorders
6. Disease and digestive system disorders
7. Disease and hepatobiliary and pancreatic system disorders
8. Disease and musculoskeletal and Conn tissue system disorders
9. Disease and skin, subcutaneous tissue, and breast disorders
10. Disease and endocrine, nutritional, and metabolic disorders
11. Disease and urinary tract disorders
12. Disease and male reproduction system disorders
13. Disease and female reproduction system disorders
14. Giving birth
15. Newborn babies and other neonates
16. Disease and blood, blood-forming organ, and immuno-logical disorders
17. Disease and myeloproliferative and neoplasm disorders, which are differentiated badly
18. Infection and parasitic disease, systemic location, or not found
19. Disease and mental disorders
20. Organic mental disorders due to the use and induction of alcohol/drugs
21. Injury, poison, and medicinal poison effects
22. Factors affecting health status and other contacts to health service
23. Medical outpatient visits

INA-DRG was initially implemented in the CHI program in 2008. A study conducted by Diah Indriani et al. at RSUP Dr Sardjito indicates that there is still a tariff discrepancy between health service real costs and INA-DRG tariffs. This discrepancy is due to inefficient medicine service and the use of laboratory resources (Indriani et al., 2013). Meanwhile, an INA-DRG study at RS Panti Waluyo Surakarta indicated a greater cost problem in reality compared to INA-DRG tariffs by 52.2% for comotio cerebri cases and 61.9% for nonhemorrhagic stroke cases, which became the study case (Pitaloka, 2011). Generally, for surgical cases, the INA-DRG cost is lower than the FFS cost, but for nonsurgical cases, the INA-DRG cost is often higher than the FFS cost, which is more traditional.

Indonesia Case Base Groups

After the INA-DRG license ended, the government developed the Indonesia Case Base Group (INA-CBG) system. INA-CBG was accepted by the Ministry of Health on January 9, 2013, after the development was carried out at the United Nations University–International Institute for Global Health (UNU-IIGH) case-mix system, which was funded by AusAID.

The basic part of the funding is the main diagnosis. The main diagnosis is the final diagnosis selected by a doctor on the patient's last bed day with the most criteria related to using resources, or what causes the longest bed day. The definition of the main diagnosis is considered fair because it is from an economic perspective, so it does not disadvantage the hospital. If there is more than one diagnosis, then the diagnosis considered eminent is the one that uses the most resources compared to the one that threatens the patient the most. The secondary diagnosis involves complications and comorbid conditions. Complications are conditions that appear during the treatment period and are considered to add to length or stay for at least one bed day. Comorbid conditions are conditions that were present at admission and are considered to add to length of stay for at least three-quarter bed day.

On the other hand, INA-CBG is also more from the patients' perspective compared to INA-DRG. INA-DRG is considered to prioritize procedures rather than diagnosis. Meanwhile, INA-CBG places more of an emphasis on the diagnostic approach than on procedures.

Furthermore, INA-CBG is applied more widely than CHI. Because this is the JKN era, INA-CBG is implemented as the claim payment quantity by BPJS Kesehatan to the reference health facility for an advanced level of service package, which is based on disease and procedural diagnosis grouping. This is stated in Decree of Minister of Health No 59 of 2014 on Standard for Health Service Tariff in the Implementation of Health Assurance Program. The number of available diagnosis groups is similar to the previous, that is, 789 inpatient groups and 288 outpatient groups. In INA-CBG, patients' conditions are divided into three conditions: severe, subsevere, and chronic. A severe condition is defined as 1–42 days of length of stay, a subsevere condition is 43–103 days of length of stay, and a chronic condition is 104–180 days of length of stay.

Tariffs for each condition are as follows:

- Severe phase tariff = Tariff of direct grouping result from INA-CBG tariff data.
- Subsevere phase tariff = Severe phase tariff + top-up payment of subsevere phase.
- Top-up payment of subsevere phase = $0.375 \times RIW \times UC \times LOSsa$.
- Resource intensity weight (RIW) is calculated with the formula: $RIW = ADL\ score/60$.
- The activities of daily living (ADL) score indicates the inability of patients to perform daily activities and is calculated with the WHO–Disability Assessment Schedule (WHO-DAS) set, which is performed on patients included in subsevere and chronic cases (Regulation of Minister of Health No. 27 of 2014 on Technical Instruction of Indonesian Case Base Group [INA-CBG] System).
- Unit cost (UC), which is by Rp 879,103.
- Length of stay (LOS), which is patient length of stay in one treatment period. For subsevere cases, the formula for LOS is $LOSsa = LOS - (LOS - 103) - 42$, with the criteria of $LOS - 103 > 0$. If $LOS - 103 \leq 0$, then it is considered $= 0$. This means LOS for the subsevere phase is none other than the difference of days between the

severe and subsevere phase lengths of stay, but it cannot exceed 103 days.

■ Meanwhile, the tariff for the chronic phase is severe phase tariff + subsevere phase top-up payment + chronic phase top-up payment. Chronic phase top-up payment = $0.25 \times RIW \times UC \times LOS$. For chronic-phase LOS calculation, $LOSk = LOS - 103$ with the criteria of $LOS - 103 > 0$. If $LOS - 103 \leq 0$, then it is considered $= 0$ because it means the chronic phase has not occurred (it has not reached 104 days).

References

Indriani, D., H. Kusnanto, A. G. Mukti, and K. Kuntoro. 2013. Dampak Biaya Laboratorium Terhadap Kesenjangan Tarif INA-CBGs dan Biaya Riil Diagnosis Leukemia. *Kesmas: Jurnal Kesehatan Masyarakat Nasional* 7(10), 440–446.

Kriegel, J., F. Jehle, H. Moser, and L. Tuttle-Weidinger. 2016. Patient logistics management of patient flows in hospitals: A comparison of Bavarian and Austrian hospitals. *International Journal of Healthcare Management* 9(4), 257–268.

Mathauer, I. and F. Wittenbecher. 2013. Hospital payment systems based on diagnosis-related groups: Experiences in low- and middle-income countries. *Bulletin of the World Health Organization* 91(10), 746–756A.

Niinimäki, T., P. Jalovaara, and E. Linnakko. 1991. Is DRG useful in orthopedics? *Acta Orthopaedica Scandinavica* 62(241 suppl), 40–41.

Permenkes No 27 Tahun 2014 Tentang Petunjuk Teknis Sistem Indonesian Case Base Group (INA-CBGs). http://www.kpmak-ugm.org/id/assets/public/PMK 27-2014 Juknis Sistem INA CBGs.pdf.

Pitaloka, S. 2011. Pelaksanaan Indonesia Diagnosis-Related Group (INA-DRG) Di Rumah Sakit Panti Waluyo Surakarta. http://etd.repository.ugm.ac.id/index.php?mod=penelitian_detail&sub=PenelitianDetail&act=view&typ=html&buku_id=52038.

Rodríguez-Rieiro, C., P. Carrasco-Garrido, V. Hernández-Barrera, A. López de Andrés, I. Jimenez-Trujillo, A. Gil de Miguel, and R. Jiménez-García. 2012. Pandemic influenza hospitalization in Spain 2009: Incidence, in-hospital mortality, comorbidities and costs. *Human Vaccines & Immunotherapeutics* 8(4), 443–447.

Rokx, C. et al. 2009. *Health Financing in Indonesia: A Reform Road Map*. Washington, DC: World Bank Publications.

Index